The Nebraska Ombudsman: Innovation in State Government

INSTITUTE OF GOVERNMENTAL STUDIES
Eugene C. Lee, *Director*

The Institute of Governmental Studies was established in 1919 as the Bureau of Public Administration, and given its present name in 1962. One of the oldest organized research units in the University of California, the Institute conducts extensive and varied research and service programs in public policy, politics, urban-metropolitan problems and public administration.

A prime resource in these endeavors is the Institute's Library, comprising more than 350,000 documents, pamphlets and periodicals related to government and public affairs. The Library serves faculty and staff members, students, public officials and interested citizens.

In addition to its traditional Library holdings, the Institute administers the State Data Program, a teaching and research collection comprising a wide variety of machine-readable data dealing with state politics, policies and institutions. It includes public opinion polls, legislative roll calls, registration and voting statistics, characteristics of state legislatures and output measures of state policies and programs.

The Institute's professional staff is composed of faculty members who hold joint Institute and departmental appointments, research specialists, librarians and graduate students from a variety of social science disciplines. In addition, the Institute is host to visiting scholars from other parts of the United States and many foreign nations.

The Institute publishes books, monographs, periodicals, reprints, reports and bibliographies for a nationwide readership. The publications are intended to stimulate research, thought and action by scholars and public officials, with respect to significant governmental and social issues.

INSTITUTE OF GOVERNMENTAL STUDIES
University of California, Berkeley

The Nebraska Ombudsman:
INNOVATION IN STATE GOVERNMENT

ALAN J. WYNER
Department of Political Science
University of California, Santa Barbara

1974

A publication of the Institute's Ombudsman Activities Project.
The research was funded by U.S. Office of Economic Opportunity Grant Number CG-9041.

Andrew S. Thomas Memorial Library
MORRIS HARVEY COLLEGE, CHARLESTON, W. VA.
93516

3 53.9782
W991n

Copyright © 1974 by the Regents of the University of California

LIBRARY OF CONGRESS CATALOGING IN PUBLICATION DATA

Wyner, Alan J
    The Nebraska ombudsman.

    "A publication of the institute's ombudsman activities project."
    1. Ombudsman--Nebraska. I. California. University. Institute of Governmental Studies. II. Title.
JK6649.04W96   353.9'782'0091   74-8958
ISBN 0-87772-199-8

$6.75

Contents

FOREWORD ix

ACKNOWLEDGMENTS xi

I   INTRODUCTION 1
      The Complaint-Handling Role 2
      Innovation in State Government 3

II   THE POLITICS OF ADOPTION 5
      Origin of the Idea 5
      Clearing the Legislative Hurdles 6
      Testimony: Redress for Citizens 7
      Testimony: Service to Legislators 8
      Legislators' Objections 10
      Arguments in Support 12
      The Problem of Uniqueness 13
      Formula for Legislative Success 15

III APPOINTING THE FIRST OMBUDSMAN 16
      The Role of "Free Money" 16
      Pressures for a Nomination 17
      A New Search 19
      Significance of the Salary 19
      Issues in the Nomination 20
      Legislative Approval 20
      Ombudsman Murrell McNeil 21

IV   EARLIER GRIEVANCE MECHANISMS IN NEBRASKA 23
      Administrative Agencies 23
      Perceptions of Administrators 24

	Public Contact and Complaints................	24
	Complaints from Penal Complex Inmates........	27
	Cases Handled by the Governor's Office.......	28
	Governor and Ombudsman: Different Caseloads...................................	30
	The Nature of Legislators' Contacts with the Public................................	30
	Types of Complaints to Legislators...........	32
	Referrals from Legislators to Ombudsman......	33
	Newspaper Action-Lines........................	34
	Campus Ombudsmen..............................	34
	City and County Governments...................	35
	Private and Semi-Governmental Groups..........	35
	The Ombudsman and Redundancy..................	36
V	THE OFFICE IN ACTION: OPERATING PROCEDURES IN THE OMBUDSMAN'S OFFICE....................	38
	The Smallest Office..........................	38
	From Federal to State Funding................	40
	Staffing and Style...........................	41
	Privacy and Access...........................	42
	Record Keeping and Case Processing...........	43
	Agency Response and Office Performance.......	46
	Operating Rules..............................	47
	Limits on anonymity......................	47
	Long-distance calls......................	47
	No requirement for exhausting alternatives................................	48
	No own-motion investigations.............	49
	Publicity for the Office and Relations with the Media..............................	50
	Mixed Results................................	52
	A Favorable Relationship.....................	53
VI	ANALYSIS OF THE OMBUDSMAN'S CASELOAD.........	54
	Number and Types of Cases....................	54
	Inquiries and Complaints.....................	55
	Jurisdiction and No-Jurisdiction Cases.......	56
	Judgment on Justification....................	56
	Types of Complaints..........................	57
	Concerning Local Governments.................	58

	Geographical Distribution of the Caseload...	59
	Method of Original Contact	61
	Elapsed Time	62
	Referrals from Legislators	63
	Factors	63
	Dangers	64
	Other Referral Sources	65
	Agencies Involved in Cases	65
	Method of Investigation	66
	Agency Level	66
	Cases from the Nebraska Poor	67
	Theory: Utility of an Ombudsman for the Poor	68
	Social Reform v. "Little" Problems	69
VII	SOME REPRESENTATIVE CASES	72
	Examples of Complaints	72
	Informational Inquiries	77
	How the Ombudsman Handles Cases	77
	Personal knowledge	77
	Legislative referrals	77
	Legislative casework	78
	Incomplete pursuit	80
	Coordination	82
	Complexity and thoroughness	82
VIII	EXTERNAL RELATIONSHIPS: THE POLITICAL AND ADMINISTRATIVE ENVIRONMENT	85
	Independence	85
	Potential Checks on Independence	86
	Funding	86
	Legislative revision	86
	Lack of gubernatorial cooperation	87
	Lack of agency cooperation	87
	Ombudsman's Reaction	87
	Evaluations by Political and Administrative Constituents	88
	Gubernatorial support	89
	Legislative support and evaluation	89
	Administrative relations	91
	Impact of the Ombudsman	92

	Participation with a legislative study committee.............................	93
	Summary...................................	94
IX	SUMMARY OF EVALUATIONS.....................	95
	Recommendations............................	97
	Staff increase.........................	97
	Keeping records and utilizing files......	98
	Legislative inquiries...................	99
	Jurisdiction............................	99
	Completeness of investigation...........	99
	Lessons from the Nebraska Innovation.......	99
	The politics of adoption................	100
	Appointing an acceptable and capable Ombudsman.............................	101
	Relations with other complaint offices...	102
	Office staffing and operation...........	102
	Caseload jurisdiction...................	104
	Options for local governments...........	104
	Relations with legislators..............	105
	Some Concluding Observations................	106

NOTES... 108

TABLE I
Nebraska Administrators' Rating of Public Evaluation (Note: Tables 2-12 and all Figures are found in Appendix I)............................ 25

FORM I
Ombudsman Information Sheet..................... 44

APPENDIX I
Figures and Tables.............................. 119

APPENDIX II
Administrative Personnel Questionnaire......... 137

APPENDIX III
Nebraska Legislature Questionnaire............. 147

APPENDIX IV
Legislative Bill 521: Public Counsel.......... 153

Foreword

For more than a decade, one of the continuing thrusts of the research program in the Institute of Governmental Studies has been exploration of the Ombudsman concept and related citizen complaint-handling mechanisms, as they have emerged in the United States and other nations. This effort has produced the substantial publication list that is reproduced on the last pages of this volume for the convenience of interested readers. The author of this book, Alan J. Wyner, is also editor of the 1973 book, *Executive Ombudsmen in the United States*.

Wyner's study of the Nebraska Ombudsman, one of the first of the state-level Ombudsmen to be established in this country, should add substantially to our still-limited, but rapidly growing recent experience with new and more effective ways of dealing with citizens who have grievances. He has followed the Nebraska effort from the preliminaries prior to adoption of the Ombudsman legislation on through to an analysis of the office's experience during its first 26 months of life. Wyner's overall assessment of the experiment is quite favorable, finding that--despite staff shortages and other expected difficulties of a break-in period--"the attempted Nebraska innovation has been successful." Moreover he comments that the office has already "moved Nebraska government closer to the goals of equity, responsiveness, and efficiency."

The Wyner contribution concludes with recommendations for future improvement in the operations of the Nebraska office. Thus the work should be of interest not only to students of the Ombudsman concept, but also to state-level executives, legislators, other policy leaders and citizens who may be considering improved ways of dealing with grievances. The experience should also be useful to local governments seeking similar objectives.

This volume is one of the final products of the Ombudsman Activities Project, which was sponsored by the Institute of Governmental Studies, financed by the Office of Economic Opportunity, conducted primarily by faculty members on the University's Santa Barbara campus, and directed by Stanley V. Anderson.

The Institute of Governmental Studies is pleased to include the monograph in its 1974 publications program. A final word of thanks is due to Institute Editor Harriet Nathan, for shepherding the manuscript through to completion, and to Catherine Winter, for typing the photo-ready copy carefully and well.

Stanley Scott

Assistant Director

Acknowledgments

This report concludes slightly over two years of research on the activities of the Nebraska Ombudsman. During this time, I have gained a greater appreciation of the difficulties citizens can have in the normal course of their interaction with our highly bureaucratized governments. Barring a dramatic reversal in the tendency toward increasing bureaucratization, it seems clear that ways must be found to ameliorate the harshness that characterizes much of the contact between citizens and bureaucracies. The Ombudsman institution provides one such opportunity.

A grant from the U.S. Office of Economic Opportunity to the Ombudsman Activities Project--located at the University of California, Santa Barbara and the Institute of Governmental Studies at the University of California, Berkeley--provided the funding for the research. Mr. Ira Kaye and Ms Pat Stolfa at OEO have been very helpful and supportive, but neither they nor OEO should be held accountable for any of the analysis or conclusions in this report. My two colleagues on the Ombudsman Activities Project, Stanley V. Anderson and John E. Moore, must be officially absolved of any responsibility for this report, but privately must be thanked for their encouragement, perceptive comments, and good humor. In helping with data collection and analysis, Glen McKay performed in his usual conscientious and thorough fashion. Somehow Sue McGuckin kept smiling as she typed the several drafts of this manuscript.

Ombudsman Murrell McNeil and his staff were very cooperative during the course of the research. McNeil's candor helped at every point.

Introduction

Starting in the early 19th century in Sweden, the Ombudsman institution has spread--first slowly, and now more rapidly--throughout the world.[1] Although there are many variations, a "classical" Ombudsman is an official selected by a legislature to investigate and make recommendations on complaints against administrative agencies, usually brought to him by private citizens. He may also initiate investigations on his own motion. Appointed by the legislature for a fixed term and at a fixed salary, he can usually be removed only by an extraordinary legislative majority, upon demonstration of adequate cause. To help achieve impartiality and independence, legislatures have made Ombudsmen relatively free from direct, politically motivated reprisals.[2] Anderson offers a concise summary of an Ombudsman's nature when he says, "The essential characteristics of the Ombudsman post require that the individual filling it be: (1) independent, (2) impartial, (3) expert in government, (4) universally accessible, and (5) empowered only to recommend and to publicize."[3]

Many types of complaint receiving offices have existed for some time, but there are at present only four Ombudsman offices in the United States that are patterned after the original Swedish version: in the states of Nebraska, Hawaii, and Iowa, and the joint office of Seattle/King County, Washington.

Hawaii holds the distinction of being the first American jurisdiction to establish an Ombudsman who possesses most of the powers and prerogatives of the Swedish version. Enabling legislation was passed in June 1967, but it took almost two years of searching and maneuvering until Herman Doi was appointed Ombudsman in April 1969. Doi has been so skillful in consolidating his position and becoming an effective instrument of complaint resolution that the other American Ombudsmen looked to him as a model during their formative periods. Shortly after Nebraska's Ombudsman began operation in 1971, the Iowa legislature approved a bill creating a state Ombudsman (called a Citizens' Aide) and thereby gave statutory existence and independence to an executive Ombudsman then working out of the governor's office. The only Ombudsman in local government that falls within the same mold as the three state offices is the joint city-county office in Seattle/King County, Washington.[4]

The Complaint-Handling Role

A fundamental tenet--both in a constitutional and moral sense--of American ideology is the right of citizens to bring complaints against their government and to petition for a redress of their grievances. Americans have employed many different avenues in pursuit of complaint resolution; classical Ombudsmen are only one such device. Thus there are literally hundreds of executive Ombudsmen in the United States. An executive Ombudsman is a complaint handling officer who has been appointed by and who serves at the pleasure of an elected or appointed chief executive. There are also some key differences in the descriptive attributes of executive Ombudsmen and classical Ombudsmen. But the functional differences are not always so clear.[5]

Elected officials have also been viewed as complaint resolvers. Mayors, governors and presidents as well as councilmen, state legislators, and congressmen continue in this role today. But the spread of the Ombudsman idea implies some substantial dissatisfaction with the more traditional complaint channels. An Ombudsman office is not a panacea, but preliminary evidence shows its utility.

This report is a description, analysis, and evaluation of the attempts to introduce the Ombudsman concept in the state of Nebraska. The idea of an Ombudsman was clearly not a new one, but Nebraska has actually implemented it. In the following chapters, I will discuss the motivation that led to the attempt, the obstacles to such innovation, the resources available to overcome the obstacles, and the degree of success achieved by the Nebraska Ombudsman. Both the motivation to innovate, and the first level of obstacles and resources used to overcome them, are treated in the context of Senator Loran Schmit's successful sponsorship of Ombudsman legislation in the 1969 Nebraska Unicameral Legislature. After passage of the legislation, attention shifts to the obstacles to success faced by Ombudsman Murrell McNeil and the resources he uses to deal with them. An examination of the Ombudsman's operating procedures and an analysis of his caseload provides evidence on this point. The final section offers an evaluation of the Nebraska Ombudsman's first two years, and a commentary on the degree to which the office has become an innovation--that is, a successful introduction of a new complaint-handling procedure into state government in Nebraska.

Innovation in State Government

Because an important clue to an understanding of the Nebraska experience lies in the innovative nature of the Ombudsman's office, some discussion of the concept of innovation is necessary at this juncture.

Advocates of a federal system of government in the United States have always argued that a multi-tiered arrangement with shared power between the governmental levels would foster experimentation in public policy. The presence of so many seats of power--in state capitols as well as Washington--would provide multiple opportunities for new ideas. Not only would there be continual stimulation from new ideas, but as a safeguard, the adoption of an untested plan in one state would limit risk in case of failure.[6]

Over the years, the American states have indeed served as laboratories for each other, and occasionally as a proving ground for the federal government.[7] Following the distinction proposed by Lawrence Mohr, the states have been *innovative* more frequently than they have been *inventive*. For Mohr, "invention implies bringing something new into being; innovation implies bringing something new into use."[8] In other words, innovation is the implementation of an invention. Invention necessarily occurs less frequently than innovation, and the truly creative act of invention is especially rare in government.[9] Invention is obviously inherently very important, but innovation occurs so much more frequently in state politics and administration that the innovative process deserves more attention.

Mohr defines innovation as "the successful introduction into an applied situation of means or ends that are new to that situation."[10] Notice the requirement for "successful" introduction; if an idea fails, then it has not been innovative. Gauging success necessitates specification of goals, development of criteria for evaluation, and analysis of data for closeness of fit between performance and goals.

Given scarce resources and the need for choice the Nebraska Ombudsman should be thought of as suggesting one among many opportunities for innovation by state government. Viewed from this perspective, Nebraska is a laboratory for other members of the federal system.[11] A review of accomplishments achieved and problems confronted in Nebraska provides examples to be emulated as well as a few errors to be avoided.

II

The Politics of Adoption

Near the end of the 1969 legislative session, Freshman Senator Loran Schmit succeeded in persuading a bare majority of his colleagues to pass legislation establishing the Nebraska Ombudsman. For Schmit, it was an important achievement, although somewhat tarnished by the ups and downs in the subsequent struggle over the appointment of the first Ombudsman, or as the legislation called the office,"Public Counsel."* Obviously, no one legislator passes legislation by himself, but in this case, his dominant leadership definitely entitles LB 521 to be known as the Schmit bill.

This chapter details the process through which Schmit maneuvered LB 521 into law. Along the route to adoption, many obstacles were faced and either surmounted or sidestepped. The political battles attendant upon adoption of the legislation provide important clues to understanding and evaluating the subsequent performance of the Nebraska Ombudsman.

Origin of the Idea

Nebraska owes the presence of an Ombudsman primarily to the insistence and perseverance of one man. This

---

*The bill, LB 521, designated the Ombudsman as "Public Counsel," a distinctly less foreign-sounding title.

episode marks one of those times in politics when government becomes innovative because a single person forced the issue.

Sometime during the late 1950's, Loran Schmit read an article about the Scandinavian Ombudsmen and immediately decided that such an institution would make a contribution in the United States at both the federal and the state levels of government. Creation of a federal Ombudsman became part of his campaign in two abortive tries for a seat in the U.S. House of Representatives. When Schmit ran for the state legislature in 1968, this time winning office, he once again used the idea in his campaign. Schmit is candid in admitting that it was probably not his advocacy of the Omubdsman that propelled him into the unicameral legislature. Yet, Schmit's own personal discomfort with the performance and sometimes the attitude of public agencies toward private citizens combined with a viable campaign issue to provide the motivation for his Ombudsman advocacy.

Both the first state (Hawaii) and the second state (Nebraska) owe their Ombudsman-enabling legislation to the work of freshman legislators. Moreover, both Hawaiian Senator Duke Kawasaki, author of the Hawaii bill, and Senator Schmit recall that their first introduction to the institution came from reading an article.[1] Written dissemination of knowledge about innovative ideas had an observable payoff. The gestation period for Loran Schmit's proposal took much longer than that of Senator Kawasaki, and Schmit used the time to become a knowledgeable and articulate proponent of the idea.

Clearing the Legislative Hurdles

LB 521 was introduced in January 1969 and was immediately referred to the Committee on Judiciary, one of whose members was the bill's sponsor, Loran Schmit. After clearing the committee with a unanimous favorable recommendation, it was sent to the Unicameral for debate and consideration. In the entire course of the bill's progress through the legislature, not one lobbyist spoke out publicly in support of or in opposition to LB 521. However, for reasons never made clear, one lobbyist for a private company apparently opposed the bill in conversations with a few senators. In a state with a usually active corps of lobbyists in the state capitol, LB 521 failed to attract attention as a priority item.

Some substantive and technical amendments to the bill were made on the floor in order to accommodate objections raised privately with Senator Schmit and objections made during the floor discussion.

The bill passed with not one vote to spare. Requiring an absolute majority of 25 of the 49 members, the final tally was 25 voting in the affirmative, 15 voting in the negative, 7 not voting and 2 absent. Senators from the metropolitan areas of Lincoln and Omaha joined with two senators from smaller cities and nine rural senators to form the winning coalition in the nonpartisan legislature. All but one of the Lincoln and Omaha senators who voted on LB 521 supported the legislation. The senators from small cities and rural areas were almost evenly split between affirmative and negative positions.

Testimony: Redress for Citizens

Senator Schmit and three others testified at the committee hearing. Two of the others were private individuals who had worked with Senator Schmit in the bill's preparation, and the third person was a resident of Lincoln who voluntarily appeared to offer support for the bill. No one spoke in opposition.

Senator Schmit's committee testimony emphasized that the goal of LB 521 was to give "the individual citizen...redress against the state government," to "humanize" government, and afford "the individual a sense of relationship with his government that he has not had in the past."² According to Schmit, providing a new channel for citizen redress and at the same time humanizing government was necessary for several reasons:

1. State government is large and complex in its organization and operation.

2. Communication between government and individual citizens is difficult.

3. Senators do not always have the time and sometimes are not qualified to help all the constituents who approach them with problems and complaints.

4. State administrative agencies treat individual citizens with much less interest and deference than they accord to senators. Consequently, the states have a responsibility to rectify problems and inequities. Schmit's reasoning closely paralleled what had, by then, become an "accepted" liturgy in academic discourse as well as in the proposals for Ombudsmen in other jurisdictions.³

Testimony: Service to Legislators

A central point of the testimony offered by Dave Evans, who had been engaged by Senator Schmit to help draft the legislation, was his suggestion that the Ombudsman would be of great help to senators. By referring citizens with problems to the Ombudsman, legislators could thereby relieve themselves of an "errand boy" function and possibly free themselves to spend more time on actual lawmaking. Evans also suggested that the Ombudsman could provide another service to legislators; his testimony on this point is worth quoting at some length.

> I think it [the Ombudsman] would provide committee research and assistance staff for the Legislature in two very

vital areas--legislative oversight and legislative overview. Legislative oversight being essentially that which has been missed, the need for more action in a certain area, the need to alter existing action when it might be found inadequate, when it might be found outdated and when indeed there is an overlap among many agencies or an overlap between the state and federal government in certain areas. Finally I think it would free the legislator and assist him in terms of creating more time for what I would call legislative overview. In other words, to sit back and reflect upon where things are going, to collect some type of research information on what the ramifications, what the implications, and what the impact of legislative proposals are upon the citizenry. The [Ombudsman] essentially could do this type of research when given such a question by the legislative body, by a legislative committee, or by a legislator himself. The [Ombudsman] could then do the necessary research and provide the legislator with the necessary facts and figures, the necessary rationale for him to either propose certain changes or for him at least to get a better, a more comprehensive overview.[4]

These comments are important because they created the clear impression in legislators' minds that the proposed Ombudsman would provide them with staff assistance.

In its traditional form, the Ombudsman was not intended to serve this function, but the Nebraska version was being modified to make the idea more appealing to a legislature that was served by a very small staff. Anticipating objections to LB 521 from some legislators,

Schmit and Evans were seeking a way to placate opponents by promising them some additional staff support from the new Ombudsman. The effect this variation produced in the Ombudsman's operations is clear: legislators often seek help from the Ombudsman on precisely the kinds of topics that Evans mentioned in his comments.

The only other topics discussed during the committee hearings were the projected size of the new office and the Ombudsman's salary. Committee members expressed concern over the possibility of creating another large governmental bureaucracy. Proponents of the bill immediately pointed out that their intention was to keep the office small, probably less than six persons. The original bill pegged the Ombudsman's salary to that of a Supreme Court justice. (In 1969, that was $20,500.) One committee member voiced the opinion that this might be too high. Apparently, he was mollified by the unchallenged assertion that a high salary was necessary to attract the caliber of person that the office demanded if it was to be meaningful.

Legislators' Objections

Senator Schmit carried the fight on the floor over the course of several legislative days. Final consideration of the bill was delayed several times, usually because Schmit agreed to amendments that required time to print and distribute. More than twice as many senators spoke in opposition to LB 521 than expressed favorable sentiments. Twelve senators participated in the floor debate.

Most arguments on the floor--both pro and con--were similar to those made in the committee hearing, although a few additional points were raised. Senators opposed to LB 521 focused their attack in four areas. First was the often expressed concern over the cost of the new office. Both the salary of $20,500 and the overall cost of the office were attacked. Senator Schmit's response was twofold. He agreed to an amendment that deleted a

specific salary and instead left the salary level to
the discretion of the Legislative Council's Executive
Board.[5] This tactic defused the immediate problem but
later the question of salary almost torpedoed the appointment of an Ombudsman. In attempting to minimize
the attack on LB 521 which was based on financial
grounds, Senator Schmit predicted an annual cost of
only $35,000. LB 521 did not appropriate any money,
but only authorized the creation of the office.

A second objection to LB 521 during floor debate
was one that has been advanced in several other states
when Ombudsman legislation has been introduced--the
belief that an Ombudsman is unnecessary and superfluous because legislators are already acting as Ombudsmen.[6] One Nebraska senator clearly expressed this
sentiment when, in speaking against the bill, he opined
that "the members of the Legislature, forty-nine of
them, representing their districts certainly represent
their people, and if they don't represent their people,
then we probably need something like this. But if they
do represent their people, they are probably the best
Ombudsman that they can get." And on those terms, he
submitted that no senator can admit that he does not
represent his constituents, so a "no" vote was in order.

The response to this "legislator as Ombudsman"
criticism took the same form as the comments Senator
Schmit made during the Judiciary Committee hearings:
It was time that legislators admit to themselves that
they are not omniscient and that they do not have the
time to fully investigate and process citizens' grievances. Moreover, the Ombudsman would not significantly
change the nature of the legislators' relationships
with their constituents.

Although mentioned on the floor only a few times,
a third objection was obviously in the legislators'
minds. It was the fear that an Ombudsman might hamper
the normal operations of administrative agencies. An
Ombudsman, so the argument went, would constantly make
burdensome requests for information and also demand

that agencies continually justify their actions. The relationship between the Ombudsman and administrative agencies would be conflict oriented. In the public's eyes, the agencies would be made to look inefficient, unresponsive, and poorly managed. This would be counterproductive and it would also be a serious setback for the cause of good government.

Arguments in Support

Senator Schmit and his supporters countered this objection by first proclaiming their belief that the vast majority of agencies, and their staffs were honest, efficient, and dedicated to performing in the best interests of Nebraskans. However, they reminded other senators, agency personnel do make mistakes and occasionally there is a bureaucrat who does not meet the high standards of his colleagues. The Ombudsman can be useful to individual citizens in the presence of either staff mistakes or the incompetent bureaucrat. Furthermore, the Ombudsman would not have the power to force agencies into changing decisions or adopting new procedures. Because he could only recommend agency action, the Ombudsman's *modus operandi* would emphasize persuasion and compromise rather than head-on conflict.

LB 521 also established other safeguards for agencies. Before the Ombudsman could make a recommendation at variance with agency policy, he was required to consult first with the affected agency. If the Ombudsman criticized an agency or a specific official in any report, the Ombudsman must also include in such reports the agency or official's reply to his criticism. The proponents of LB 521 were trying to suggest that any adverse commentary about an agency would be amply balanced by the agency's rebuttal.

The Problem of Uniqueness

The last objection raised during floor debate was the hardest to counter. Several senators voiced concern that the Ombudsman was a unique and untried idea. They were suggesting, by inference, that Nebraska should not be used as an "experimental" testing ground. As one senator complained, "There's really no place where you can look to see how the thing works."

At the time of this floor debate, Hawaii had passed its Ombudsman legislation but had not yet appointed its first Ombudsman. Senators in opposition to LB 521 apparently were not impressed with Senator Schmit's recital of the Ombudsman's success in foreign nations. The comments about uniqueness bring to mind Jack L. Walker's conclusion after studying the process of innovation adoption in American states:

> In all cases...the likelihood of a state adopting a new program is higher if other states have already adopted the idea. The likelihood becomes higher still if the innovation has been adopted by a state viewed by key decision makers as a point of legitimate comparison.[7]

Opponents of LB 521 in the Nebraska Legislature were unimpressed with reference to foreign experience, and furthermore they would not have been impressed by the Hawaiian example if that Ombudsman had already been a glowing success. For some Nebraska senators, Hawaii proves as irrelevant by way of example as any Scandinavian country.

Discomfort with uniqueness is difficult to fight because there are no substantive grounds upon which to base a counterattack. This objection leads the discussion away from the merits of the proposal at hand and into an arena in which each legislator's attitude about taking risks becomes primary. One senator, favorable to LB 521, expressed his sentiments about innovation this way:

> I don't know why, when anybody has a good idea, or when some people have good ideas, just because it involves a change or doing something different people are opposed to it. Now, if we tried this [the Ombudsman] for a couple years and it doesn't work, the world isn't going to fall apart. You can change it. So, I say let's give it a whirl and see what happens. It might help the people a little bit.

Notwithstanding this senator's willingness to innovate, when decisionmakers are faced with innovative efforts they are dealing with uncertainty. And, "under conditions of uncertainty, they cannot assign probabilities for the occurrence of particular consequences, or at least these probabilities cannot be assigned with any degree of confidence."[8] Willingness to take risks, and an assessment of the motivations and capabilities of the innovation's sponsor, become paramount factors in the decisionmaking process.

After the verbal give and take ended, the first recorded vote asked for the Unicameral's preference on LB 521 with an "emergency clause" attached. This clause declared an emergency and would have had the bill take effect immediately. With the emergency clause attached, LB 521 received 26 votes, far short of the two-thirds majority required for emergency legislation. On the next vote, for LB 521 without the emergency clause, the needed 25 votes were secured and the bill was sent to the governor for his action.

At the time LB 521 was passed, Governor N. Tiemann and the Unicameral were at odds over other important policies. The legislature had just overridden several gubernatorial vetoes. In this atmosphere of conflict, and with a less than overwhelming affirmative vote on

LB 521, the governor showed no inclination to sign the bill into law quickly. After conversations with several senators, including Senator Schmit, and on the very last day on which Governor Tiemann could sign the bill before it would become law without his signature, Governor Tiemann attached his name to LB 521. He had been persuaded that the Ombudsman was a good idea, that it was not an attempt to install a politically motivated critic of his administration, and that the bill ought to be kept separate from conflicts with the legislature over other matters.

Formula for Legislative Success

Several points can be summarized from the legislative struggle over LB 521. Senator Schmit carried the day and he probably did so for at least two reasons. First, it is apparent that Schmit had a keen understanding of both the major parts and the fine nuances of the bill. He also knew how to deal with his supporting and opposing colleagues on different parts of the legislation. Second, as is not uncommon in state legislatures, Schmit relied upon personal relationships with many senators and counted on his friends to support his idea even if they were not in total agreement with it. On this particular occasion, enough senators rejected the "uniqueness" objection and were persuaded to allow Nebraska to assume an innovative role.

As will be shown later, every one of the major objections to LB 521--cost, legislators' desire to serve as Ombudsmen, concern over agency prerogatives, and uniqueness--has played a part in helping define the initial operating guidelines for Murrell McNeil.

Appointing the First Ombudsman

The official Nebraska *Legislative Journal* contains the following bland entry for May 5, 1971: "The Executive Board herewith submits the name of Murrell McNeil to the position of Ombudsman." In the subsequent vote, McNeil was unanimously approved as Nebraska's first Ombudsman, although 11 senators did not vote on the nomination.[1] To say that the vote was anti-climactic would be a gross understatement. So much uncertainty and controversy over the appointment plagued the almost two-year interval between passage of LB 521 and McNeil's nomination that establishment of the office became problematical. The final version of LB 521 gave the Executive Board responsibility for nominating an Ombudsman and setting his salary. The board was required to send the nomination to the Unicameral, where a two-thirds vote was necessary for confirmation. As the drama over the appointment unfolded, important players were the Executive Board, Senator Schmit, and newly elected Governor J. J. Exon.

The Role of "Free Money"

Neither Senator Schmit nor any other supporters were trying to write a law tailored to the appointment of any specific person as the first Ombudsman. For example, none of the amendments to the original bill seemed motivated by any plans to make it easier or harder for any particular individual to occupy the post. Schmit's priority was to pass the legislation and then worry about the appointment. Without trying to second guess the proponents of LB 521, some of the opposition's fears about the bill might have been allayed if the legislative "grapevine" had been informed that a widely respected individual was in line to become the first appointee. If such a person had been available, his personal qualities might have eased the bill's passage, as had been the experience in Hawaii.[2]

The Executive Board's mandate to nominate an Ombudsman was devoid of any reference to salary or to an operating budget for the office. Two powerful members of the Executive Board had voted against LB 521, and the board did not seem in any hurry to make the nomination. The question of finances was settled in May 1970, when the United States Office of Economic Opportunity agreed to underwrite almost totally the cost of the Ombudsman's salary and office expenses. OEO promised a grant of $70,530 for the first year's operation, with the understanding that the office would be eligible for a similar and final grant the following year. The federal government made available twice the amount of money that Senator Schmit had predicted would be sufficient.[3] As with so many other activities of state governments, the carrot of federal money was dangled before the Nebraska Executive Board. That the legislature finally implemented the Ombudsman office must be attributed in great measure to this source of "free money."

Pressures for a Nomination

The Unicameral did not meet again until January 1971. This eight-month time span reinforced the Executive Board's already slow pace toward a nomination, inasmuch as the nominee could not take office without legislative approval. Senator Schmit, on the other hand, was anxious for the Executive Board to make the nomination in the Spring or Summer of 1970 so that the appointment could be considered at the very beginning of the new legislative session. Schmit was also concerned that, unless action on the nomination was forthcoming soon after the federal grant, the whole issue might get placed in hibernation, never to awaken.

Prodded by Schmit and a few of his supporters on the Executive Board, serious consideration of a nomination finally began in late 1970. At that time, the board apparently settled upon the nomination of a former statehouse newspaper reporter who was then working on the Washington staff of a United States Senator from Nebraska. The only apparent impediment to the actual nomination was a dispute between this individual and the board over salary--a difference of approximately $5,000. As might be expected, word of the pending nomination spread to legislators and to the governor. Legislators' reaction were enthusiastic. More than two-thirds of the legislators signed a letter endorsing the nomination. Governor Exon privately expressed some hesitation about the nomination because he was concerned that the potential nominee wanted the job only to further the U.S. Senator's reelection. Governor Exon, not a member of the senator's political party, was naturally worried about such a prospect. After receiving assurances, including those of Senator Schmit, that the potential nominee would act in a non-political manner, Governor Exon issued a statement strongly endorsing the man.

The mounting pressure on the Executive Board for this individual's nomination apparently violated its own sense of propriety. After all, they were charged with the nominating responsibility. Nothing happened for several days until the potential nominee, probably annoyed at all the commotion over his nomination, and unwilling to accept the lower salary offered by the Executive Board, withdrew his name from consideration. Rather than pursue the matter, the Executive Board took his withdrawal at face value and indicated that the search would begin anew.

A New Search

During this second phase of the search, the Executive Board interviewed more than 20 persons without discovering one who was acceptable. Then they tried again, only to run headlong into Senator Schmit. The board approached Schmit with a small list of new names from which they were prepared to select the nominee. Schmit did not find anyone on the new list who filled his expectations, and he made that view clear to the board. Not wanting to provoke a fight with Senator Schmit on the floor when the legislature considered the nomination, the board once again renewed its search.

At this point in late Spring 1971, the Executive Board turned to a man literally under its nose. After consultation with Senator Schmit, the nomination was offered to Murrell McNeil, who at that time was working as a researcher for the Legislative Council. After a few days of hesitation and thought, McNeil accepted the nomination with a salary set at $17,500.

Significance of the Salary

The furor over the Ombudsman's salary, which started with the introduction of LB 521 and only ended with McNeil's nomination, necessitated a compromise. The final amount was less than that received by Supreme Court Justices but considerably more than the $12,000 figure once mentioned during the committee hearings. The dispute over salary was about more than money. Salary denotes status and importance, and that was what motivated the controversy. To be effective, an Ombudsman must have status and perceived importance, and McNeil's salary gives him both. His salary compares favorably to that paid such officials as the Secretary of State, the State Treasurer, the Auditor of Public Accounts, and other similar executive officials. Since his appointment, McNeil's salary has been raised to account for inflation, but he maintains parity with executive officials like those just named. His current salary is $18,400.

Issues in the Nomination

The struggle over McNeil's nomination illustrates the intensely personal nature of such decisions. At issue were the inter-personal relationships between the key actors. Schmit's stature was such that, although he was not on the Executive Board, he was able to veto a proposed nomination. The dispute between the board and their first nominee was as much a controversy over how much money that particular man was worth as it was a disagreement over the value of an Ombdusman. Governor Exon, whose cooperation with any new Ombudsman was important, had doubts about the motivations of this individual. And there is some indication that certain executive officials were upset at the possibility that an Ombudsman—untested and foreign—might make more money than they. Given all this, it is not surprising that the nomination process was slow and sometimes painful. Furthermore, the agony over the nomination was well known to Murrell McNeil, and it has had some impact on his operating style. At a minimum, it has made him sensitive to the need for good rapport with legislators.

Legislative Approval

A large turnover in legislators occurred between the 1969 and the 1971 legislative sessions. Fifteen freshman senators were sworn in at the start of the 1971 session. This turnover meant that almost one-third of the legislature that received the Executive Board's nomination of Murrell McNeil was not present during the debate and vote on LB 521. Twelve of the newcomers favored McNeil's appointment, while three chose not to vote.

What of those senators who voted against LB 521 in 1969? Eight were no longer in the Unicameral and the remaining seven voted to approve McNeil. Four senators who favored the legislation chose not to vote upon the confirmation.

When all was said and done, Murrell McNeil became Nebraska's first Ombudsman on May 5, 1971, by a vote of 38-0.

Ombudsman Murrell McNeil

At the age of 54, Murrell McNeil had already completed two careers--one of long and one of short duration--when the legislature appointed him as Ombudsman. McNeil retired as an Army Lieutenant Colonel in 1963 after 22 years in the service. His second career started in 1966 when Governor Tiemann appointed him State Tax Commissioner. Although he was not reappointed to the position in 1970 by newly elected Governor Exon, during the four years of his tenure McNeil became one of the most publicly visible state administrators.

It was his fortune to become tax commissioner at the very time that Nebraska first imposed a sales and income tax on its citizens. Starting almost from scratch, McNeil built and organized bureaucratic machinery necessary to collect these new taxes. Through extensive media coverage and endless speaking at public gatherings, McNeil became a well-known official. And, of course, the nature of his job meant that he had close contact with legislators.

By all reports, McNeil emerged relatively unscathed from four years as tax commissioner. In an editorial shortly after his appointment as Ombudsman, the Lincoln *Star* commented favorably on McNeil: "There is no question of McNeil's competency or of his public sensitivity, so essential for this job. This was proven in the highly volatile office of tax commissioner which he occupied under Governor Tiemann."[4]

McNeil does not hide the fact that he was originally skeptical about establishing an Ombudsman in Nebraska, and he did not think LB 521 necessary. Reflecting his role as an administrator at the time LB 521 was passed, McNeil then saw the Ombudsman as someone who would be constantly second-guessing state government agencies.[5] Between 1969 and his appointment, especially in those hectic few days when he was considering the Executive Board's offer of the nomination, McNeil came to realize that he had neither understood the intent of the legislature nor the duties of the Ombudsman. After some personal investigation and thought about the job, he finally decided that the key role of the new Ombudsman would be to reconcile differences between citizens and agencies. As long as he could do this without wielding a heavy stick and using fear as a tactic he was eager for the job.

McNeil took office on June 1, 1971, convinced that the basic concepts behind the new office were correct; the people of Nebraska needed an Ombudsman, and in the process, both the people and their state government would be served. The first two years would test his new optimism.

Earlier Grievance Mechanisms in Nebraska

The new Ombudsman did not step into a vacuum in the field of complaint processing. Nebraskans already had several channels through which they could voice their grievances about government. Although most of these channels lead directly to administrative agencies or elected officials, some quasi-governmental groups (e.g., community action projects) as well as private organizations also received complaints about state government. For a better appreciation of the Ombudsman's work, it is appropriate to pay some attention to related grievance mechanisms before undertaking a detailed examination of Murrell McNeil's office.

Administrative Agencies

All state agencies, and especially the larger ones that have more extensive contact with the public, receive complaints or inquiries implying a complaint. Some agencies, such as the Department of Public Welfare, have developed a formal grievance procedure replete with specific forms and channels through which the forms must be forwarded. The Department of Public Welfare reports that appeals, which are complaints about agency decisions, have doubled in the last few years. Other agencies, usually the smaller ones, handle complaints and inquiries on an ad hoc basis, varying with the nature of the problem and the availability of staff personnel.

Perceptions of Administrators

A survey conducted during the summer of 1973 allows an examination of some perceptions held by Nebraska administrators. The questionnaire was mailed to a randomly selected sample of middle level and top level bureaucrats in the state government.[1] Respondents were asked for their perceptions about the way in which the public views their agency and for an indication and appraisal of their agency's complaint-handling procedures.

Most respondents believe that the public assesses their agency's performance as "adequate," while some administrators perceive the public's evaluation as "very good." When asked to describe the public's opinion of all administrative agencies in general, there is a noticeable decline in "very good" ratings with a corresponding increase in "adequate" ratings. The individual administrator's greater pride in his own agency as opposed to the rest of the executive branch is evident. (See Table 1.) One conclusion to be derived from these ratings is that Nebraska administrators see themselves working in public organizations that have the support of their fellow citizens. Very few administrators sense that the public holds them in poor regard.

Examining administrators' responses to a series of questions about their contact with the public should illuminate some rationale for these perceptions. Respondents felt that they spent a considerable portion of their time in contact with the public. ("Contact" includes anything from meeting personally with a citizen to writing a letter to a citizen.) Forty-two percent of the respondents reported that public contact occupied at least one-half their work time; 69 percent indicated public contact took 30 percent or more of their time.

Public Contact and Complaints

The vast majority of the public contacts by administrators did not involve complaints. Respondents were

Table 1[a]

Nebraska Administrators' Rating of Public Evaluation of Agencies

Which one of the following statements most accurately describes the opinions of Nebraskans....

	Toward your agency	Toward all administrative agencies
Citizens feel we (they) are doing a very good job	29.5%	10.9%
Citizens feel we (they) are doing an adequate job	61.5	80.8
Citizens have no opinions	5.8	5.1
Citizens feel we (they) are doing a poor job	1.3	0.6
Citizens feel we (they) are doing a very poor job	0.0	0.0
No response	1.9	2.5
	100 % (N=156)	99.9%[b] (N=156)

[a] Tables 2-12 are found in Appendix I.

[b] Does not total 100%, due to rounding.

asked to estimate the percent of their public contact that dealt with complaints from citizens. Eighty-two percent of the respondents estimated that 20 percent or less of their time spent in public contacts involved complaints.

The lack of extensive complaint handling by most administrators can be interpreted two ways. Either the complaint-handling process in the agencies is highly centralized, with only a few administrators receiving and processing complaints, or Nebraskans do not complain very much when interacting with administrators. A definitive assessment of the alternative explanations for the low complaints/public contacts ratio is impossible because of inadequate data (e.g., a survey of Nebraskans to learn about their inclination to complain is missing from our data base). However, there is some evidence from the survey of administrators to indicate that complaint processing is somewhat centralized, and, therefore, not many administrators have contact with the public by receiving citizen complaints.[2]

Most complaints from citizens are not valid, according to the respondents. To the extent that the complaint-handling process in agencies is centralized, most respondents are not in a position to offer firm opinions about the percent of valid complaints; their knowledge of complaints may be second hand. Keeping this caveat in mind, 62 percent of the respondents estimate that ten percent or less of the complaints received are valid; 74 percent of the respondents feel that 30 percent or less of the complaints are valid.

In summary, the administrators are saying that although they have extensive contact with the public, only a fraction of those contacts involve citizens' complaints. Moreover, when citizens bring complaints to their agencies it is the administrators' opinion that most of the time the complaints are not justified. Looking a little ahead in this analysis, a later section will show a much higher percent of justified or partially justified complaints lodged with the Ombudsman.

Complaints from Penal Complex Inmates

The State Penal Complex, located in Lincoln, is under the jurisdiction of the Department of Institutions. The clients of this agency are special in that they are all confined. It should not be any surprise to learn that inmates of the Penal Complex have complaints. These grievances are directed at both the conditions within the institution and at the legal system outside the prison. Due to recent interest in complaint resolution within prisons, an attempt was made to learn about the procedures used in the largest prison in Nebraska.[3]

For the last two years, a part-time complaint officer has been working as part of the warden's personal staff. Persons who have held this position are either current or retired members of the prison staff. Working about 12 hours per week, this official processes complaints that prisoners have forwarded to him via the prison's internal mail system. An average of approximately ten complaints per week are received. Most complaints are about the quality of food preparation, the adequacy of laundry services, or the conduct of prison officers. Because no formal records are kept, it is impossible to ascertain the resolution of cases or the legitimacy of the complaints. In an interview with Ed Scarborough, then serving as complaint officer in 1972, he ventured the opinion that the vast majority of complaints were unjustified; there is no practical way to verify this.

Inmates may send uncensored and unopened mail to several outside individuals, including the governor and the attorney-general but not including the Ombudsman. As the Ombudsman-enabling legislation was originally introduced, the Ombudsman would have become one of those with whom prisoners could have privileged communication. The original wording stated,

> A letter to the Public Counsel from a person in a place of detention or in a hospital or other institution under

the control of an administrative a-
gency shall be immediately forwarded,
unopened, to the Public Counsel.

This section was deleted during committee deliberations at the insistence of a few senators who felt that prison officials were strongly against it. Despite the absence of privileged communication with the Ombudsman, prisoners can still write to him. Mail from prisoners to the Ombudsman would be opened and inspected for contraband like any other letter, but according to official prison policy no letter would be censored. This system of mail handling probably guarantees that a letter will leave the prison uncensored, but it is possible to bring pressure on those inmates who are known to have complained.

During the entire first year's operation, the state Ombudsman did not receive any correspondence from inmates of the State Penal Complex. At the time Ed Scarborough was interviewed, he admitted being unaware of the activities of the state Ombudsman and he had had no contact with Murrell McNeil. Inmates did not initially correspond with McNeil either because they were not aware of his existence or because they felt he would not help. It is also possible that the internal prison complaint mechanism was adequate. Some evidence that the latter two explanations were not the case comes from the gradual increase in the number of inquiries and complaints McNeil has received from inmates during 1973.

Cases Handled by the Governor's Office

Detailed records of complaints are not kept by the governor's office. Even without precise data, it is obvious that the governor is a focal point for citizens who have a problem concerning state government.

When the Ombudsman first went to work, some members of the governor's staff felt that as the Ombudsman became an established and well-known entity many Nebraskans

who would otherwise contact the governor's office would
send their complaint to Murrell McNeil. After two years
of existence, the Ombudsman has not made any difference
in the volume of or type of complaints received by the
governor, according to a staff aide. Although these impressions can never be substantiated unless the governor's office is inclined to keep more accurate records
of complaint intake, the perceived lack of drop-off in
gubernatorial complaints prompted a closer look at the
nature of cases handled by the governor's office.

Examining a sample of the governor's mail revealed
several interesting points of comparison with the Ombudsman's caseload.[4] Most of the correspondence dealt
with matters of policy--pending or recently enacted law.
Much of this type of citizen input, if not all of it,
is irrelevant from an Ombudsman's point of view. The
specific inquiries and complaints about administrative
matters are referred to the appropriate agencies, and
the governor's office receives a copy of the replies
sent by agencies to citizens. Most agencies handle
this referred mail quickly. The typical turn-around
time was 7-10 days, and only rarely did an agency take
more than two weeks. The governor's office usually
does not do anything other than file a copy of the a-
gency's letter. There is no follow-up to see if, in
fact, the agency performed in the way it promised the
citizen it would.[5]

One feature that often distinguished the mail kept
and answered by the governor's staff rather than being
sent to an agency was the specificity of inquiry or
complaint. The more specific the letter, then the more
likely that it would be referred to an agency. As a
consequence, the governor's staff found itself often
replying to "unanswerable" complaints, e.g., "My taxes
are too high and I want you to do something about it."
Replies to these complaints take the form of generalized
statements about good government and the need to spend
public money wisely.

Governor and Ombudsman: Different Caseloads

In conclusion, it appears that the governor's office and the Ombudsman handle different kinds of caseloads. First, most of the Ombudsman's caseload is about specific problems, not generalized grievances or comments about the appropriateness of state laws. Second, the mail coming to the governor's office is primarily from citizens who are making their first contact with state government about the issue at hand. Where citizens often use the Ombudsman as a court of last resort, this clearly was not the case with the governor's office.

Understandably, the governor prefers not to refer complainants to the Ombudsman. Such referral might appear rude and smack of a runaround. When the governor refers a citizen to an agency, he can tell the agency when he wants the return letter sent over his own name and when it is to go out on the agency's stationary. This kind of control would not be possible with an independent Ombudsman. For this and other reasons, there have been only a handful of referrals from the governor to the Ombudsman. These referrals occurred in a few selected cases where the governor's staff felt that because of the partisan implications of the complaint, the citizen would be more likely to accept the finding of the Ombudsman than the conclusion reached by the governor. To put the matter more bluntly, the governor did not want to accept the responsibility for giving the citizen a reply that would be unfavorable to the complainant.

The Nature of Legislators' Contacts with the Public

Nebraska's forty-nine senators sit in the nation's only unicameral state legislature. Because of their relatively small number, one would expect them to have high public visibility. If this assumption is true, then senators should be the recipients of many constituents' complaints. During June 1972 and June 1973, all Nebraska legislators were mailed a questionnaire designed to assess the nature of the contact they had with constituents. The two sets of questionnaires are not cumulative--although the same questions were asked both times--because there were eleven new senators in 1973. The response rate in 1972 was 71 percent (35) and in 1973 it was 69 percent (34).[6]

	Percentage of Legislator's Contacts with Citizens that are:	
	1972	1973
Opinions on issues or suggestions for legislation	50%	67%
Requests for legislation	31	21
Complaints about state government	15	9
Other	4	3
	100% (N=35)	100% (N=34)

When the Nebraska Legislature was in session, the average number of contacts per week that senators estimate receiving from citizens was 43 (N=33) in 1972 and 62 (N=32) in 1973; when the legislature is not meeting, the average number per week dropped to 13 in 1972 and 11 in 1973.[7] Legislators were asked to indicate the nature of these contacts, presumably combining both in- and out-of-session perceptions.

Legislators' perceptions about the nature of their contacts with the public changed from 1972 to 1973. Of the changes, the decline in the percentage of complaints is of special interest. Nebraskans are either complaining less to legislators because they are sending their complaints to other persons or perhaps they are complaining less to all potential complaint recipients. In this context, it should be noted that the Ombudsman's total caseload declined during his second year of operation, but the percentage of cases which were complaints rose slightly. Available data do not permit a clear cut conclusion about whether the decrease in legislators' complaints (as a percent of their total contacts) has any connection with a change in the Ombudsman work load.

Types of Complaints to Legislators

When legislators were asked to identify the most common types of *complaints* received (out of the total amount of contacts), they did not name specific agencies against which citizens brought grievances. Rather, they spoke in more general terms, and appeared mentally to be grouping the complaints into categories. For instance, instead of specifying that he received complaints about abusive behavior by a particular official of a particular agency, the legislator would simply indicate "harassment by agency personnel." Legislators could indicate more than one kind of complaint and they are summarized and arrayed below:

	1972	1973
Taxes and/or the cost of government	30%	18%
Agency regulation or administration of regulations, or agency personnel	27	32
Pending or recently enacted legislation	22	23
Communication: Inability to know where to go or to whom to speak about a problem	11	10
Miscellaneous	10	17
	100% (N=56)	100% (N=69)

Averaging their responses about complaints only, legislators in 1972 reported that 34 percent of the complaints received about state government were valid, while the figure rose to 43 percent in 1973. The questionnaire suggested that a valid and justified complaint occurred when the state government made an error or when an individual had been treated improperly by an agency.

Looking ahead to subsequent analysis of the Ombudsman's caseload, it is worth noting at this point that 52 percent of the *legislators' complaint caseload* in 1972 and 41 percent in 1973 were in areas that seldom come to the Ombudsman's attention--namely, taxes and legislation. To a great extent, Nebraskans are using their legislators and their Ombudsman as different kinds of complaint channels. This point, plus the fact that only a small percentage of the senators' public contact involves citizens' complaints, offers evidence to refute the criticisms of the Ombudsman advanced during legislative consideration of LB 521--namely, that legislators are already serving as Ombudsmen.

Referrals from Legislators to Ombudsman

Of course, the data suggest some overlap between the Ombudsman's work and the legislators' citizen contact caseload. Both the requests for information from legislators and complaints other than those about taxes and legislation are also within the Ombudsman's bailiwick. Another way of highlighting the overlap is to look at referrals from legislators to the Ombudsman.

Thirty-three senators responded to the question on referral. In the 1972 survey, 33 senators reported that they referred a total of 360 cases to Murrell McNeil, and in 1973, 31 senators reported a jump to 568 referred cases. This averages approximately 11 per legislator in 1972 and 18 per legislator in 1973.

Discounting problems of recall with this type of question, but keeping in mind that all senators did not reply, it is somewhat surprising that legislators' perceptions of referral exceed the Ombudsman's records of referral by a factor of two in 1972 and by a factor of 2.5 in 1973. The discrepancy probably occurs for at least two reasons. First, the Ombudsman (correctly) does not complete a case record form for every legislative referral because many are minor and can be dealt with in a matter of minutes. Second, legislative impressions of the Ombudsman's office are so favorable that legislators probably think they are using this highly-thought-of office more than in fact is the case.

Newspaper Action-Lines

One of the major Lincoln newspapers (the *Evening Journal*) and the large Omaha metropolitan paper (the *World-Herald*) have "action line" types of columns, and to the best of our knowledge these are the only two papers in the state that include this service. From even a casual examination of the columns, it is easy to conclude that they do not carry many inquiries or complaints about state government. Those state government complaints that are found in these columns tend to be questions like "Why is the crime rate so high?"--questions or implied complaints that are general and that often defy precise answers. Neither paper has referred citizens directly to the Ombudsman nor have they themselves used the services of the Ombudsman.

On one occasion the Action Line editor of the *World-Herald* referred a citizen to the state Welfare Department who in turn suggested that the person contact McNeil. After the case was closed McNeil informed the editor of his findings.

Campus Ombudsmen

Both the Lincoln and Omaha campuses of the University have Ombudsmen appointed by their respective chancellors after nomination by a joint student-faculty-administration search committee. Both of these men serve large constituencies--over 25,000 at Lincoln and over 10,000 at Omaha. During the 18 months that the Lincoln campus Ombudsman has been in office, there have been several occasions where he has worked cooperatively with Murrell McNeil. There has been no contact between the Omaha campus Ombudsman and McNeil.

Some of the complaints and inquiries the Lincoln campus Ombudsman receives deal with the state government rather than the University. In these cases, he will often handle the matter himself, especially when it is relatively simple, and at his discretion notify McNeil. Many of the Lincoln campus Ombudsman's state government cases can be resolved quickly after one or two telephone calls. McNeil's caseload is thereby reduced by whatever number of these complaints the University Ombudsman pursues on his own.

City and County Governments

In both the two large metropolitan areas of Nebraska, there are governmental officials who function as complaint officers. A staff member for the Lincoln Mayor and one for the Omaha Mayor handle all complaints directed toward these offices. Likewise, a staff member for the Douglas County (Omaha) Board of Commissioners processes complaints for the board. None of these staff members handles complaints on a full-time basis; their primary responsibilities are in other areas. On occasion, McNeil has worked with the Lincoln Mayor's office.

Private and Semi-Governmental Groups

Private interest groups, especially those that represent Nebraska farmers, often serve as mediators between aggrieved citizens and the state government. Some of these groups, such as the American Civil Liberties Union or the semi-public Legal Aid Societies, will also instigate legal action on behalf of a citizen. Social action agencies such as the National Association for the Advancement of Colored People or the OEO funded Community Action Agencies routinely process complaints about government, although many of these complaints are directed toward local government, e.g., County Welfare Departments.

The Ombudsman and Redundancy

The lesson that should be learned from this brief excursion into the field of complaint processing in Nebraska is simple: the Office of Ombudsman was created and it must live in an environment in which Nebraskans have some other opportunities to express their complaints against government. The extent to which the Ombudsman duplicates, complements, or replaces these other complaint channels must become part of the evaluation of the Ombudsman's performance.

It is possible that the Ombudsman could duplicate other complaint opportunities but no evidence that suggests duplication was uncovered. A descriptive term that seems more apt is "complement."

The Ombudsman should be characterized as providing similar opportunities for registering complaints against state government. There is no doubt that overlap exists between the services McNeil offers and those available from others such as legislators and the governor. In a word, the Nebraska political arena has some built-in redundancy. As Martin Landau has forcefully argued, redundancy in any system is an important organizational element and is deeply rooted in American political and constitutional traditions.[8] Landau concludes:

> redundancy serves many vital functions
> in the conduct of public administration.
> It provides safety factors, permits
> flexible responses to anomalous situa-
> tions and provides a creative potential

for those who are able to see it.
If there is no duplication, no
overlap, if there is no ambiguity,
an organization will neither be
able to suppress error nor generate alternative routes of action.
In short, it will be most unreliable
and least flexible, sluggish, as we
now say.[9]

It would be unfortunate if the Nebraska Ombudsman, or any Ombudsman for that matter, completely replaced other major complaint channels. The danger of such complete centralization rests in the potentially disastrous consequences in the event of failure.[10] For example, allowing Nebraskans to voice complaints about state government only through the Ombudsman's office--to illustrate an extreme complaint handling centralization--assumes a constantly and effectively functioning office. But the resulting case overload would make it impossible for the office to function effectively and preserve the values associated with the Ombudsman concept.

The goal should be an office that provides unique visibility to a citizen's right to voice a complaint. This should attract a significant number of meaningful cases, while at the same time neither taking over all the complaint functions in the jurisdiction nor merely duplicating what others are doing. In others words, the ideal is redundancy of opportunity to complain but not complete redundancy of actual operating functions.

V

The Office in Action: Operating Procedures in the Ombudsman's Office

The Ombudsman has articulated several goals to guide his office's operating procedures: (1) Keep the office small, easily accessible, and relatively inexpensive; (2) develop an efficient office routine; and (3) acquaint Nebraskans with the office's potential. Murrell McNeil's activities during the first two years have moved the office a considerable distance toward accomplishment of these goals. This chapter outlines some of those activities.

The Smallest Office

Flying in the face of the traditional American pattern of large, complex bureaucratic structures, but entirely in keeping with the spirit and intent of Ombudsman legislation, McNeil has kept his office staff small. Any Ombudsman would take pride in the headline in the newspaper that serves the small community of Plattsmouth, Nebraska: "Ombudsman Smallest State Office." In addition to himself, McNeil employs one full-time administrative assistant, one part-time typist, and a lawyer who spends about one-third of his work week in the Ombudsman's office.

McNeil handles almost all of the casework himself, relying upon the lawyer for legal advice or legal research. He utilizes his administrative assistant for investigation and research on cases and for some secretarial functions. With few exceptions, every letter addressed to a citizen is actually dictated and signed by McNeil. This is also true of the vast majority of the correspondence with state agencies.

During these first two years of operation, the Ombudsman has deliberately chosen to be involved in virtually every aspect of almost every case. While time-consuming, this procedure has allowed McNeil to gain an unchallengeable understanding of the gamut of problems Nebraskans experience with state government. Furthermore, his constant attention to the casework has forced him into extensive contact with agencies, and this has had beneficial consequences for both McNeil and the agencies. McNeil has learned even more than he already knew about administrative decisionmaking, and agency personnel have had a first-hand look at the head of the institution that many bureaucrats may have feared or opposed.

However, the main advantage of McNeil's style accrues to the citizen. Every inquirer or complainant knows that the Ombudsman will personally handle his case. This contrast to the normal routine in the typical agency can not fail to create a refreshing aura.

During the 26-month period from May 1, 1971 to June 30, 1973, McNeil has recorded expenses totalling $87,261:[1]

Staff	$67,094
Operating expenses	7,906
Supplies and materials	560
Travel expenses	1,971
Capital outlay	6,243
In-kind services provided by the state (office space and utilities)	3,487
	$87,261

Because salaries comprise such a large percentage of any budget, McNeil's personal attention to the caseload with the consequent small staff permits the office to operate on a modest budget. The resemblance between Senator Schmit's original cost estimate of $35,000 per annum and the actual expenditure of approximately $40,000 per annum is striking. McNeil is apparently trying to show legislators that an effective Ombudsman program can be managed without an exorbitant budget.

From Federal to State Funding

As the Ombudsman's two-year grant from the Office of Economic Opportunity drew to a close, it became apparent that a considerable amount of money would be left unspent--appoximately $50,000. McNeil was initially informed by OEO that he would be able to apply one-half of the unspent money to his fiscal year 1973-74 budget, with the remainder being returned to the federal treasury. After extended negotiation and several administrative staff changes at OEO, McNeil was permitted to keep the entire $50,000. Before the OEO decision to permit retention of the $50,000 was assured, McNeil had requested an operating budget of approximately $48,000 from the state. His budget request was submitted to the legislature as part of the operating budget for the Legislative Council, which is the organizational home for the Ombudsman.

The request for state funding was an important hurdle, which when cleared would provide a good indication about the Ombudsman's acceptance as a regular and continuing part of state government. Allocation of state money would provide an important clue about the degree of success the innovation had achieved. Refusal to support the Ombudsman with state money could be taken as an indicator of failure.

With neither debate nor dissent, the legislature unanimously approved McNeil's budget request. Permission to keep the $50,000 in federal money means that McNeil will not spend very much, if any, of the state allocation during the coming fiscal year. If in order for an idea to be considered an innovation, it must be "successfully introduced," then state funding of the Ombudsman shows at least a minimal level of success. The Nebraska Ombudsman is an innovation because it survived. In fact, it did more than merely survive. Comparing the narrow one-vote margin by which the office was established with the unanimous agreement to provide state money for the office strongly suggests that McNeil's office has passed the first tests of a new institution and now moves to a new level of support and opportunities.

Staffing and Style

There are clear opportunity costs attached to McNeil's style of thorough personal attention to the caseload. For instance, despite McNeil's active efforts at publicizing the office, a state as large as Nebraska with both large metropolitan and dispersed rural areas presents an ominous challenge to anyone disseminating information about a new governmental service. The need for publicity is almost endless. Rather than spend as much time as he does on the casework, McNeil could have chosen to delegate some of that responsibility and spend even more time on publicity. Another cost to McNeil's style is the possibility that the quantity of work will dampen his motivation to spend as much time as might be required on the truly complicated cases. This does not seem to have happened, but it is a possibility that must be watched.

This discussion obviously involves some second-guessing: the Ombudsman has chosen a staffing pattern that forces his explicit and personal attention to an amazing amount of detail. Because time is limited, his choice precludes other activities. It is our opinion that McNeil has wisely chosen to immerse himself in the casework, and in the long run, he will be a more effective Ombudsman because of it. However, in the near future, the Ombudsman may want to re-examine his own time schedule and decide whether the office still benefits from his constant personal attention to every case or whether additional staff would free him to concentrate on other, and perhaps newer, tasks. Use of his statutory power to initiate his own investigations is precisely the kind of new activity that additional staff would permit. (This question is discussed in more detail in a subsequent section.) The newly voiced formal legislative support for the office, as seen through the budgetary allocation, provides the opportunity to add an additional staff member under a favorable political climate.

Privacy and Access

After a few temporary locations, the Ombudsman is now settled in a convenient place on the main floor of the state capitol building. The internal office configuration guarantees a somewhat removed and private office for McNeil. Citizens walking in with a problem can be ushered back to McNeil's office where the surroundings convey a genuine sense of privacy. The Ombudsman's physical location thus meets the twin needs of easy accessibility and privacy for citizen interaction.

At several points during the preceding year, Murrell McNeil has evaluated the desirability of opening another office in Omaha. At each instance, he concluded that a second office was not feasible; his judgment seems sound. Two offices, while perhaps easing access for some Omaha residents, would have presented management and budgetary problems that were better left aside during the early life of a major new institution.[2] The issue should not be closed permanently, however. Omaha represents the state's largest concentration of people, and an office in proximity to those residing in the metropolitan area may have great utility. Evidence from Lincoln indicates that proximity is important. Almost one-third of the Lincoln citizens who used the Ombudsman's services made their initial contact in person at the office. Timing for the opening of an Omaha office should be left strictly to the Ombudsman's judgment, but it is appropriate to review periodically the need for a second office.

Record Keeping and Case Processing

The "Ombudsman Information Sheet" is the internal form used to record relevant information and provide a permanent history of each case (see Form 1). After initially entering the name and address of the citizen as well as the substance of the inquiry or complaint, the official updates the Information Sheet in chronological fashion as the case proceeds. Following the final disposition of a case, the Ombudsman records his recommendations and judgment about the justification of a complaint. The file is then permanently stored in the office.

Actually, the office keeps three types of permanent files. Each complaint is assigned a unique number, using a scheme that includes the date on which the citizen brought the complaint to the Ombudsman. Filing by case number cross-referenced to the complainant's name permits easy retrieval. Inquiries are filed by name and are not given a case number. A third file records all the cases according to the state agency involved.

An effective record keeping system in an Ombudsman's office should meet these criteria:

1. A complete, accurate record of the citizen's original question or complaint.

2. A complete, accurate, and prompt notification to the appropriate operating agency.

3. A check on, and perhaps a control over, the length of time required for an agency's reply and the quality of the reply.

4. A complete and accurate response by the office to a citizen, and within a reasonable time span.

FORM 1

Ombudsman Information Sheet

CASE NO. _____
(Complaint only)

DATE OF INQUIRY   TAKEN BY   ASSIGNED TO

NAME OF INQUIRER_____ ____WRITTEN
                                      ____PHONE CALL
ADDRESS_____   ____VISIT

TELEPHONE (R)_____ (B)_____

TYPE: _____COMPLAINT   _____NO JURISDICTION

           _____INFORMATION   _____NO JURISDICTION
                                          BUT ASSISTANCE
                                          PROVIDED

SUBJECT:_____

SUBSTANCE OF INQUIRY OR COMPLAINT:

AGENCY:_____

CHRONOLOGY:

COMMENTS AND RECOMMENDATIONS:

FOR NO-JURISDICTION CASES ONLY

    _____Federal
    _____County
    _____Municipal
    _____Other Sub-divisions
        of Government

    _____Legislative Issue
    _____Issue before Courts
    _____Private Matter between
        Individuals
    _____Issue Involving Governor
        or His Immediate Staff

OMBUDSMAN RECOMMENDATIONS

    _____Agency Should Explain Issue to Citizen or Resolve
        Problem
    _____Ombudsman Will Explain Issue to Citizen or Resolve
        Problem
    _____Change Recommended in Agency Administrative Rules
        or Procedures
    _____Change in Law Will Be Recommended
    _____Personnel Action Recommended
    _____Agency Should Modify Its Decision in Case

FOR COMPLAINTS WITHIN JURISDICTION

    _____Justified
    _____Partially Justified
    _____Unjustified

COMPLAINANT NOTIFIED _____

DATE CLOSED_____DISCONTINUED_____

CHRONOLOGY (Continued):

COMMENTS AND RECOMMENDATIONS (Continued):

5. An organizational memory enabling the office to (a) prepare special and annual reports, and (b) evaluate its own performance.

The procedures and forms used in McNeil's office allow the Ombudsman to meet the above criteria. But in addition to the simple mechanics of record keeping, an effective office staff must have motivation to make the record keeping system work to its full advantage. For instance, it would be insufficient to merely have a form that indicated the date an agency was notified about a complaint if the office staff did not also develop a routine for periodic appraisal of the status of cases sent to agencies for their comment. Moreover, an Ombudsman who wants to maintain his independence must evaluate an agency's reply and not just accept it pro forma.[3]

Agency Response and Office Performance

There are two key links in the list of record keeping criteria: assessment of an agency's response and evaluation of the office's performance. The other criteria can be routinized and usually performed by a competent office staff, but these two tasks are crucial and require the Ombudsman's personal judgment. Yet at the same time, they are prime candidates for short shrift because of time pressures, and the common human tendency to procrastinate or even ignore difficult situations.

McNeil's office is a model of bureaucratic efficiency in meeting the routinized criteria. With the exception of a few cases where the Ombudsman probably should have demanded a more thorough agency response, McNeil has extracted reasonably high quality agency responses. Agency responses are normally detailed and to the point; when they have been evasive, McNeil has often asked for more information.

The last criterion of an effective record keeping system (number 5 above) emphasizes the importance of organizational memory. McNeil's office has the memory but it has not been used to its fullest potential advantage. The office has not prepared any special reports, such as an evaluation of complaint trends in specific areas; the annual reports are sufficient but do not provide a depth of analysis that would permit thorough evaluation of the office. A more detailed and documented annual report would also serve the function of forcing its author--the Ombudsman--to make a more in-depth evaluation of office trends and caseload characteristics.

Operating Rules

Limits on anonymity. Several operating rules adopted by McNeil have had an impact on the office's character. For example, the office will accept anonymous complaints provided they are not directed against specific agency personnel. Anonymous complaints may prove valid and therefore a remedy may be found. However, McNeil refuses, correctly in our view, to accept complaints lodged against individuals unless the complainant fully identifies himself. In such cases, the Ombudsman will protect the complainant's identity if he desires and if it is possible. To help preclude unfounded and malicious attacks on state employees, McNeil insists that the complainant reveal his identity. As a matter of record, McNeil has received only two anonymous complaints to date.

Long-distance calls. Serving such a widely dispersed clientele presents logistical problems. For instance, those citizens not residing in Lincoln who wish to speak with McNeil on the telephone must place a long-distance call. In some cases, this cost may be prohibitive. For the period May 1971 to June 1973, 17 percent of the cases from other than Lincoln were originated by telephone. The Ombudsman has an out-going Wide Area Telephone Service (WATS), but not an in-coming one. On telephone calls that McNeil judges will take more than three minutes, he asks the caller to hang up, whereupon McNeil immediately returns the call and continues the conversation. Therefore, the most any citizen would have to pay is the cost of a three-minute call to Lincoln.

Not only is an in-coming WATS line expensive (about $12,000 a year for equipment and staff) but, more importantly, a free long-distance telephone call to the state capitol would provide temptation that could plague the Ombudsman. The office would probably receive a large number of requests for information about all kinds of programs and activities that, strictly speaking, it should not handle. Yet, it would be too rude to turn down these requests for information. The caseload would increase with an in-coming WATS line but the number of significant, important cases probably would not. A few senators tried to persuade their colleagues to authorize an in-coming WATS line for the Ombudsman, but the move was eventually defeated on grounds of cost and amid reservations about the need for it.

No requirement for exhausting alternatives. It would be possible for the Ombudsman to interpret LB 521 in a way that would require citizens to exhaust all their potential administrative remedies before the Ombudsman accepted jurisdiction of a case. Not only would such an interpretation be impractical, but if strictly enforced, it would seriously erode public support for the office. Under this strict interpretation, the Ombudsman would ask a citizen to trace, in detail, all his attempts to resolve the issue. Many would not remember or perhaps understand all that had happened; they would be frustrated in their attempt to secure the Ombudsman's aid because he would often send them to an agency in order to guarantee exhaustion of all possible remedies. Furthermore, one of the reasons the Ombudsman was established, and one of the reasons many citizens use the office, is precisely to abate or avoid the buck-passing, the "No, you're in the wrong office" routine that afflicts many governmental agencies.

Murrell McNeil never tells a citizen that he is in the wrong office. An effort is made to help everyone who contacts the office, regardless of the citizen's previous efforts (or lack thereof). This "open door" policy means a greater caseload and probably more problems for the office, but it is entirely within the spirit of the Ombudsman institution and for that reason is encouraging. The Ombudsman must, however, be alert to the potential danger of taking all comers. He may at some point find that the "extra" work caused by those citizens who have not exhausted other possible remedies causes a less than adequate treatment of other cases. In other words, an open door policy may require additional staff.

No own-motion investigations. Another operating rule that helps define the office is McNeil's choice not to exercise his power to "investigate...on his own motion any administrative act of any administrative agency." Again, it is primarily a matter of economy. Rather than start his own investigations, McNeil concerns himself with the cases brought to his attention by citizens. The day-to-day pressure from these cases more than keeps him busy. "Own motion" investigations are options that can be pursued only with the time that would be created for McNeil by additional staff. The experience of the Seattle Ombudsman with own-motion investigations illustrates the enormous amount of time they consume.[4]

In terms of impact on the administrative process, special investigations of specific issues or suspected problems may produce more constructive criticism than any one particular citizen-initiated case. With the possibility of a greater payoff, own-motion investigations, by their very nature, carry greater risks to a new Ombudsman's acceptance in state government.

In this type of investigation, it soon becomes apparent that the Ombudsman himself and not an aggrieved citizen is the initiator, and he cannot use his statutory obligation to pursue citizens' complaints as the rationale for examination of an agency's facilities or documents. Furthermore, the Ombudsman will not start his own investigation unless he thinks the issue is important. In the event that his original suspicions prove warranted, the ramifications of suggested charges could be significant. To put it bluntly, it could get very hot in the kitchen and, unless the Ombudsman is prepared to take the heat, he is better off staying away.

While own-motion investigations can be important and should be undertaken when warranted, McNeil (or any Ombudsman) should choose the issue carefully. Nebraskans deserve to have McNeil's expertise used to improve state government, but the political realities also deserve respect; no purpose is served by an Ombudsman severely restricted in his ability to resolve individual complaints because he has made agencies hostile by inappropriate own-motion investigations. McNeil is a master of judging propitious moments and he will undoubtedly initiate a special investigation when an important issue is at hand, the time is ripe, and staff resources are adequate to undertake them without displacing attention from individual complaints.

Publicity for the Office and Relations with the Media

The Ombudsman is extremely conscious of the need for disseminating information about the office, and employs a wide range of publicity techniques. Publicity is vital; whether the different techniques are equally beneficial is doubtful and should be assessed. For instance, citizens using the office could be asked their initial source of information about the Ombudsman's services.

It is hard to imagine the Ombudsman, with his present staff, doing more to publicize the office. Time spent publicizing means time away from the casework, and while the office is being further publicized, the caseload would presumably increase as a result of the publicity.

Newspaper coverage has been good. In large part, McNeil receives coverage in the state's newspapers because of his speechmaking activities. Most papers, especially those in small towns or rural areas, will publish a small story announcing McNeil's forthcoming presence and will carry a story about his remarks. His office and his activities have clearly aroused the interest of the state's newspapers. In addition to the articles generated from his speeches, several long feature stories have also appeared. Associated Press stories have received the widest circulation; the same feature story may appear in six or eight different papers. Newspapers in Lincoln and Omaha have also run feature stories on the office, including a long story and interview in the Omaha *World-Herald*'s Sunday magazine. Special interest publications such as the *Nebraska Farmer* have also featured the office.

McNeil has also made use of the electronic media, and has appeared on several radio and television interview programs. During legislative sessions, the state's Educational Television Service broadcasts a weekly program about state government and McNeil participates regularly. He has also succeeded in having Nebraska's radio stations read prepared "spot announcements" on the air.

His frequent speaking engagements are time consuming, especially with distances being so great; it is approximately 400 miles from Lincoln to Scottsbluff. McNeil has spoken to dozens of "service" organizations: Rotary, Kiwanis, Lions, Chamber of Commerce, and others. These occasions permit him to spread the word about the office on a more personal note than can be accomplished through the media.

In addition, he has addressed the staffs of several Community Action Program agencies in the state. These agencies, and their clientele, are ordinarily difficult to reach effectively. An example will make this point clearer. The Ombudsman has had several contacts with the major leaders of the community action programs in Lincoln. Yet, when staff from the Ombudsman Activities Project spoke to a few active participants in two of that city's anti-poverty organizations, it was apparent that the Ombudsman and his services were largely unknown. This suggests that, within his resources, the Ombudsman should strive to penetrate the top layer of CAP agencies and reach individuals who are in daily contact with poor Nebraskans.

Mixed Results

Of three other publicity tactics, two are known to have had payoff, although one of those was disappointing. Placing posters and brochures in the state's libraries is a good idea in theory, but there is no indication whether it has worked. McNeil's practice of giving each cooperating senator a handful of the Ombudsman's business cards has had more evident results. The card contains all the information necessary to contact McNeil. Several cases have come to the Ombudsman via this route.

The disappointing, though partially successful, publicity effort consisted of a mailing to school superintendents in the state inviting them or relevant teachers in their districts to contact McNeil for any material they might want to use in classrooms. Of the few hundred superintendents on the list, only a handful replied.

One approach that might offer some promise of educating and informing Nebraskans about the Ombudsman's office is writing a newspaper column. The late Dayton, Ohio Ombudsman, Theodore Bingham, wrote a column three times a week in which he discussed recent cases (omitting names) as well as the functions of his office. Although this type of activity is time consuming, it does guarantee the Ombudsman continual access to the press, and can acquaint Nebraskans with both the capabilities and limitations of the office. At the moment, the Nebraska Ombudsman is too busy for such an undertaking, assuming the press would be interested, but the opportunity should not be forgotten.

A Favorable Relationship

A mutually beneficial relationship has developed between the media and the Ombudsman. McNeil has been appropriately aggressive in seeking out the media and using them to inform Nebraskans. On the other hand, McNeil has frequently been approached by reporters and broadcasters in search of a story or an interview. As nearly as can be determined by reading Nebraska newspaper stories and editorials about the Ombudsman, McNeil enjoys the confidence of the media. For instance, the Lincoln *Star* editorialized that "The Nebraska Ombudsman program, as it looks now, was a wise experiment."[5] Newspapers support his office; that support is not only helpful for informing Nebraskans but also for letting legislators know that McNeil has sufficiently impressed the media that they also support his activities.

VI

Analysis of the Ombudsman's Caseload

Number and Types of Cases

For the 26-month period May 1971 through June 1973, the Ombudsman recorded 1,526 cases. Between May 1, 1971 and June 30, 1972, there were 854 recorded cases, averaging 61 per month. The subsequent 12-month period produced 672 recorded cases, declining to an average of 56 per month. These figures include only those cases for which records have been kept. Several hundred contacts with the office during this time were not recorded because they were simple questions and requests, and often related to non-jurisdictional matters, e.g., "Where do I get a city (state) map?" The Ombudsman has estimated that between 300 and 400 phone calls a year are of this variety.

Another important qualification must be considered; caseload does not necessarily equal workload. The amount of time and intellectual effort demanded by different cases can vary enormously. Where one case may be satisfactorily completed in one morning with a few phone calls, another case may require many days of nearly constant attention. It is useless to compute average amounts of time or money expended to complete a "typical" case; the range is too large. Thus, a simple comparison between the Ombudsman's first and second year caseload may lead to erroneous conclusions. Specifically, a decline in numbers of cases in the second year does not *a priori* mean a decline in the workload. If, for instance, the number of complicated, time-consuming cases increased during the second year, then the decline in caseload may have accompanied increased workload. This possibility will be explored further in a later section.

Inquiries and Complaints

Cases are categorized into two main types: inquiries and complaints. Fifty-nine percent of the cases were complaints, and the remainder inquiries. Although a strict reading of the Ombudsman legislation might suggest that only complaints ought to be within the office's jurisdiction, this would be an unwarranted and impractical interpretation. The Nebraska Ombudsman was created to assist citizens when they have problems with the state government; often these problems are articulated as questions about how to resolve the problem. Furthermore, many questions are implied complaints. If a citizen asks, "Why didn't I get my tax refund last month?" he may, by implication, be alleging an unwarranted slowness on the part of the bureaucracy--that is, a complaint. For these reasons, the Nebraska Ombudsman has properly allowed his office to answer citizens' questions. As McNeil is aware, the inquiry side of the caseload must not be allowed to consume a disproportionate share of time. So far it has not done so.

Figures 1 and 2 present a picture of the caseload as it developed over the 26 months. (All tables and figures discussed here appear in Appendix I.) The notable increase in caseload during the first three months of both 1972 and 1973, as seen in Figure 1, is attributable to the legislature's being in session. Thirty-five percent of the Ombudsman's total caseload originated during those six months. Not only do legislators, while in Lincoln, refer cases more often, but the state's news media naturally give more attention to state government during the session. Citizens are therefore more cognizant of state government and more likely to raise questions or bring complaints forward. As Figure 2 demonstrates, complaints outnumbered inquiries in all but three months, but during the January-March periods, complaints far outstripped inquiries.

Jurisdiction and No-Jurisdiction Cases

The categories of cases handled by the Ombudsman are shown in Table 2 (see Appendix I). Several interpretive comments are in order. The Ombudsman's jurisdiction is technically limited to administrative agencies of the state government, and a case, inquiry or complaint, is classified as "no-jurisdiction" if the subject pertains to anything else. McNeil usually provides some form of assistance for individuals presenting "no-jurisdiction" complaints or inquiries. Often he will write a letter to the proper office or public official; in no-jurisdiction cases that appear critical, he will often do whatever he can. Those no-jurisdiction cases in which McNeil does no more than advise the citizen of the proper place to file a case are categorized as "no-jurisdiction, no assistance provided." Yet, even here, McNeil is, of course, helping by providing proper direction.

Table 2 collapses the two-year period; the only change between the first and second year was a slight decline in jurisdiction inquiries and an increase in no-jurisdiction inquiries. Although slight, this trend is somewhat disquieting. As time passes, Nebraskans should become better equipped to voice complaints and inquiries that fall within the Ombudsman's jurisdiction. The need again becomes obvious for continuous publicity that stresses both the areas in which the Ombudsman does not have jurisdiction as well as the areas in which he does.

Judgment on Justification

Table 2 also indicates the Ombudsman's judgment about the justifiability of the complaints within his jurisdiction. Looking only at jurisdictional complaints, the table shows that 40 percent are justified, 15 percent are partially so, and 45 percent are not justified, according to the Ombudsman's judgment.

Examining types of complaints (as opposed to inquiries) brought to the Ombudsman, Table 3 classifies complaint type for both jurisdiction and no-jurisdiction complaints. These complaint types are based on the allegations of the citizen making the complaint. Most of the jurisdictional complaints allege an inadequacy in administrative procedure or an inappropriate administrative opinion. Apparently, very few citizens are involved in a dispute with an agency over factual matters. A sizable number of no-jurisdiction complaints allege the presence of either an inadequate or unfair law or relate to a private legal matter.

Types of Complaints

To further clarify different types of complaints citizens bring to the office, Table 4 provides an opportunity to assess the justification of complaints that fall into the eight complaint categories. Of most interest are those within the Ombudsman's jurisdiction. (In those cases outside his legal jurisdiction, his ability to pursue a complaint is often seriously limited. Therefore, no-jurisdiction complaints, while perhaps suggestive, are not accorded the same importance in this analysis.) Table 4 clearly shows that most complaints judged partially justified or (completely) justified allege an inadequacy in administrative procedure. In this instance, a procedure is defined as any operating rule or regulation, formal or informal, that administrative agencies employ in decisionmaking. The Ombudsman's tasks in this kind of complaint are to assure himself and the citizen that the procedure is fair and that it is being applied in an equitable manner.

The largest number of unjustified complaints alleged an inappropriate administrative opinion. This is not surprising, because the Ombudsman's job should not lead him to second-guess administrators who have followed lawful procedures and who have arrived at a decision which, while reasonable, differs from that desired by the citizen. As long as the Ombudsman is satisfied that a reasonable exercise of discretion has been invoked--with due regard for mitigating circumstances--he must necessarily find for the agency. Such a finding, however, does not prevent him from offering advice, off the record, to the agency or to the citizen, about ways to avoid further conflict.

While small in number--9 percent of the total complaints--those complaints alleging some form of misconduct by public officials have a slightly higher than average level of justification. Of the 38 complaints within the Ombudsman's jurisdiction that alleged misconduct, 53 percent were either totally justified or partially justified. Apparently, Nebraskans do not find many specific public bureaucrats about whom they feel obliged to complain, but when they do lodge such a complaint, the odds are slightly better than even that the complaint is at least partially justified.

Concerning Local Governments

One further note about the no-jurisdiction caseload that the Ombudsman received; almost 38 percent dealt with Nebraska local government: counties, cities, and other subdivisions of government (see Table 5). And of those, fully 73 percent were complaints. Because these complaints are beyond his legal jurisdiction, McNeil does not make a judgment about them. However, there is no reason to suspect that the rate of justified complaints for local government would be substantially less than the rate for state government; in fact, there are some indications that the justification rate is probably higher for local government.

It is apparent from the data that many Nebraskans are unhappy with some aspects of their local government, and they are turning to the state for redress. Given this trend, the Nebraska Ombudsman might look closely at the developing experience of the Iowa Ombudsman, who has just assumed jurisdiction over local government in addition to the Iowa state government. Although now is not perhaps the proper time, it is conceivable that in the future the Nebraska Ombudsman's jurisdiction should be extended to include local government, as is the case in Hawaii and Iowa.

Geographical Distribution of the Caseload

While it is obvious that Nebraskans from every part of the state availed themselves of the Ombudsman's services, the data permit specific examination of the geographic origin of the caseload. We should not expect to find an exact correspondence between the state's population distribution and the Ombudsman's caseload distribution, but any gross disparities would be worrisome.

Table 6 displays the geographic origin of the Ombudsman's caseload, compared to the distribution of Nebraska's population. The small cities are slightly over-represented and the rural areas slightly under-represented in the total caseload. Yet, the similarity between caseload and population is striking, and it confirms the impression that the Ombudsman is serving the entire state.

When the data are further refined, it becomes clear that within each of the three major population categories--metropolitan, small cities, and rural--there are some differential uses of the Ombudsman. Omaha contributes substantially fewer cases per capita than does Lincoln;[1] Scottsbluff and North Platte citizens are using the office on a per capita basis slightly less than other small cities; and the rural counties of Sioux,

Banner, Garden, Hooker, Thomas, Blaine, McPherson, Logan, Wheeler, and Stanton are using the office significantly less than other rural counties.

The point is worth repeating: no magic value should be attached to a precise correspondence between caseload and population distribution. Less than perfect correspondence does not mean that the Ombudsman is any less important or effective. And to put the obverse, a perfect correspondence between caseload and population distribution would not necessarily mean that the Ombudsman is working at an effective level. The best use to which such data can be put by the Ombudsman is to stimulate a greater effort at publicity in the under-represented areas, and if time is a problem, to provide less publicity in those areas over-represented. More publicity in Omaha should receive a high priority.

As mentioned earlier, during the first three months of 1972 and 1973, the Ombudsman's caseload took a dramatic upswing. It was also hypothesized previously that greater attention to state government during those legislative session months was a likely cause of the increase. Figure 3, which shows that most of that increase came from rural areas, leads to the impression that rural Nebraskans are more sensitive to state government matters during legislative sessions than are their counterparts in the small cities and metropolitan areas.

While each of the three geographical categories submitted approximately the same number of complaints as a percentage of the total cases from each category, for some unexplainable reason, the complaints from the small cities were judged to be either completely or partially justified with slightly greater frequency than the complaints from either the metropolitan or rural areas. It would be pure speculation to attempt an explanation.

Method of Original Contact

Nebraskans have relied upon the postal service to bring most of their complaints or inquiries to the Ombudsman's attention. Citizens contacted the office by letter in 55.9 percent of the cases, by telephone in 25.3 percent of the cases, by personal visit in 18.1 percent of the cases, and by a combination of the three in .7 percent of the cases. As the following data show, the method of original contact is not related to whether the case is a complaint or an inquiry; citizens were more likely to bring forth complaints than inquiries, irrespective of the method employed.

Contact the office by mail: 40% inquiries
                                                       60 complaints

Contact the office by telephone: 48% inquiries
                                                       52 complaints

Contact the office by personal visit: 36% inquiries
                                                       64 complaints

Likewise, the method of original contact is not related to the justification of a complaint. Therefore, the Ombudsman must treat all complaints, regardless of method of contact, in the same manner. LB 521 provides that the Ombudsman "may prescribe the methods by which complaints are to be made...." Cases conveyed by mail are the most convenient for any Ombudsman because they permit him more complete control over his daily time schedule; he can read the mail when he is ready. Conversely, when a citizen telephones or presents himself at the office, the Ombudsman must make himself or his staff available within a short time. The Nebraska experience clearly shows that a significant minority of citizens who desire help from the Ombudsman prefer either to visit or to telephone. Murrell McNeil's policy of letting the citizen choose his own method of contact, rather than a method more convenient for the Ombudsman, is appropriate and commendable.

Elapsed Time

Delay is anathema to the Ombudsman's office. Quick resolution of a case is a primary goal. A speedy resolution of most cases requires not only efficient operating procedures in the Ombudsman's office, but also the cooperation of the appropriate agencies. The Nebraska Ombudsman works quickly, and he has obviously received excellent cooperation from the bureaucracy.[2] Table 7 gives firm evidence of the speed with which Nebraskans can expect a final disposition.

Two characteristics, embedded in the data of Table 7 but not readily apparent, deserve mention. During the second year, McNeil increased the percentage of cases completed in less than three days from 52.5 percent to 56.6 percent. This slight increase in speed is evidence of further experience; providing the workload and staff remain as they are now, it is hard to see how the percentage of cases closed so quickly can be increased much more.

The cases that take the longest to complete are the justified complaints: only 29 percent are completed in less than three days. Justified complaints are often complicated, and require extensive communication among the agency, the Ombudsman, and the aggrieved citizen. Rapid handling of casework does not necessarily demonstrate the Ombudsman's effectiveness, but it gives evidence that the Nebraska Ombudsman is meeting one important goal of his office--providing quick service to citizens with no more delay than is absolutely necessary.

When LB 521 was debated on the floor of the legislature, one objection suggested that the Ombudsman would interfere with the "normal" activities of the administrative agencies. While far from providing definitive proof of this objection's falsity, agencies respond to McNeil's requests for information with a speed that suggests they are not trying to hinder the Ombudsman by delays. They might do so if they viewed him as unnecessarily meddlesome. On his part, McNeil has often stated that less than complete cooperation from agencies is a rarity.

Referrals from Legislators

One gauge of the Ombudsman's acceptance by the legislature is the large number of cases that senators have either presented themselves or that result from referrals by senators. Twenty-six percent (387) of the Ombudsman's caseload came to his attention from a senator, either directly or by referral. (During the second year, legislative referrals climbed to 33 percent.) During fiscal year 1971-72, 37 of the 49 senators used his office at least once; and during fiscal 1972-73, the number rose to 43. Several senators have responded to suggestions (during committee hearings and floor debate on LB 521) that the Ombudsman could help legislators do research on policy matters. Although as a practical matter, it is difficult for McNeil to refuse such requests, this kind of work was not envisioned by LB 521.[3] The high percentage of his caseload that comes from legislative referral shows that the Ombudsman is not seen as a threat to legislative-constituent relations. On the contrary, legislators seem to have learned that McNeil can be helpful in dealing with constituents. However, the large number of legislative referrals, and the increase from 21 percent of his caseload in 1971-72 to 33 percent in 1972-73, provide some grounds for consideration of McNeil's legislative relationships. Does McNeil work too closely with the senators? Is a disproportionate share of his caseload coming from legislators?

Factors. Several reasons account for McNeil's legislative referrals.[4] First, and perhaps most important, is McNeil's reputation and personal relationships with the senators. Throughout Nebraska state government, but especially in the legislature, McNeil is widely respected as a man of unquestioned integrity. What this means for legislators is simple: McNeil can be trusted to keep confidences and to not become involved in the legislature's internal power struggles.

Confidence in McNeil works with two other factors to increase his legislative referrals. One is physical proximity. McNeil's office is in the capitol building, and adjacent to senatorial offices. Finally, the Nebraska legislature does not provide much staff or secretarial support for itself. The lack of personal staff encourages senators to refer constituents to McNeil.

Dangers. The dangers of a high legislative referral caseload are two-fold. First, as the percentage of referred cases gets higher, the proportion of citizen-originated cases must necessarily decline. The Nebraska Ombudsman was intended to be directly available to private citizens. For this direct access to be a reality, the Ombudsman must continually publicize his office and encourage individuals to voice their complaints directly to him. If the public "learns" during the Ombudsman's formative years that it is helpful to speak with their senator first, then a fundamental character of the office would be changed, contrary to the intention of LB 521.[5]

The second problem is the possibility that legislative referrals will be treated preferentially. As has been shown, McNeil processes all his cases quickly; legislative referrals are not getting unusually fast handling. With only a few exceptions, the caseload resulting from senatorial referral is no different in substance or number of justifiable complaints than the caseload coming directly from private citizens. When necessary, McNeil has not hesitated to tell a senator that one of his constituents' complaints is not justified.

Ultimately, McNeil is responsible to the legislature. By encouraging senators to use his office, McNeil has been able to earn their approval while at the same time maintaining the degree of independence required by the Ombudsman concept. An Ombudsman is independent if he can say "no" to legislative and executive officials, as well as citizens, when his judgment tells him it is required. As long as this condition is fulfilled, McNeil can remain independent.

Other Referral Sources

Other than senators, no other source has referred more than a handful of cases to the Ombudsman. In addition to the legislative referrals, 124 cases were referred rather than directly initiated by the citizen. These referrals came from sources such as the lieutenant governor, private lawyers, agency personnel, and individual citizens. Including all sources, referrals account for 521 cases or 34 percent of McNeil's total 26-month caseload.

Agencies Involved in Cases

Examining the extent to which McNeil's caseload deals with each state agency indicates the subject matter of his caseload as well. State government is organized along functional lines, e.g., the Roads Department is responsible for state roads and the Department of Revenue collects taxes.

It is not surprising to find that those Nebraska agencies with the highest number of employees, and concurrently the greatest daily contact with the public, also are the subject of the greatest proportion of the Ombudsman's caseload. The following eight departments were involved in 51 percent of the 952 cases that fell within the Ombudsman's jurisdiction: Education, Health, Labor, Motor Vehicles, Public Institutions, Public Welfare, Revenue, and Roads. The remainder of the jurisdictional caseload was distributed among boards, commissions, minor state offices, and the University. For the eight departments, the percentage of either partially or totally justified complaints is virtually identical to the partially or totally justified complaints for the entire caseload. Although they are bigger, these eight departments fare no worse than the smaller state agencies.

Method of Investigation

Just as citizens have their choice of the means used to contact the Ombudsman, McNeil can choose his form of contact with agency personnel. Reliance upon the telephone is overwhelming. In 77 percent of the 795 cases for which data are available, the Ombudsman relied upon the telephone to establish contact with the appropriate agency.[6] He personally visited the agency in 9 percent of these cases, wrote a letter in 4 percent and in the remaining 10 percent used some combination of telephone, visits, and mail.

Agency Level

As a result of his previous service as tax commissioner, Murrell McNeil has many acquaintances within state government, many of them at the top of administrative agencies. Apparently McNeil feels comfortable going to the upper hierarchical levels of agencies, because in 47 percent of the 579 cases where data are available, the Ombudsman dealt with the head of an agency, a personal assistant to the head or the number-two man in the agency. In 23 percent of the cases, McNeil discussed the case with middle-level management in an agency, e.g., a bureau chief, and in 30 percent of the cases, a staff member at a lower level (often in an operational job) was contacted. The Ombudsman's pattern of going directly to the top may seem unusual in light of other Ombudsmen's experience, but the circumstances of McNeil's background make this a likely route for him to pursue.

Cases from the Nebraska Poor

The Ombudsman's office attempted to identify all cases in which "the poor" were requesting service. Feeling that it would be inappropriate to ask citizens their income and assets, the office has relied upon a less offensive but also less accurate guide to identify poverty-level clients. All clientele who are on some form of public assistance or who are eligible are classified as poor. This scheme probably underestimates the number of poor people who use the office, but without further prying into individuals' financial records it must suffice.

Using the above criteria, the Ombudsman served 153 poor citizens, who comprise 10 percent of his total caseload.[7] According to the U.S. Bureau of the Census, 13.1 percent of all Nebraskans have incomes less than the poverty level.[8] Compared to the geographic origin of the entire caseload (see Table 6), a much higher percentage of poor than not-poor came from metropolitan areas. Conversely, a lower percentage of poor than not-poor came from small cities and rural areas.

Tables 8 through 10 compare the poor and not-poor with respect to their types of cases, their types of complaints, and the days needed by the Ombudsman to close the cases. The poor bring a higher percentage of complaints as opposed to inquiries, and a higher percentage of their complaints are judged unjustified.

There is an important explanation for the higher unjustified rate. The agency most frequently involved (but by no means the only agency) in cases from the poor is the Department of Public Welfare. Most of the unjustified complaints are about welfare payments, rules, and procedures. State law vests county welfare agencies with enormous discretion and McNeil's jurisdiction does not extend to county welfare agencies. McNeil's jurisdiction is limited to those few instances where the Department of Public Welfare has rules and procedures governing local welfare administration. Most of the welfare complaints that McNeil discusses with state welfare personnel are unjustified in the sense that no violation of law, procedure or equity has been perpetrated, but rather that the complainant's ire has been aroused by the discretionary action of a local welfare official--something neither the state agency nor McNeil can do much about. These complaints are considered within his jurisdiction for our coding purposes because of the potential involvement by the state agency.

Tables 9 and 10 show a distinct similarity between the types of complaints levied by the poor and not-poor and the time required to close both poor and not-poor cases. With the exception of the Department of Public Welfare, the poor bring cases to the Ombudsman concerning other state agencies in roughly the same proportion as those from not-poor. More than welfare troubles the poor.

Theory: Utility of an Ombudsman for the Poor

What little attention has been given to the relevance of the Ombudsman institution to poor Americans has focused almost entirely on the limitations and capabilities of Ombudsmen in local government.[9] Of what relevance for the poor is a state Ombudsman? Given a choice, which would be more beneficial to the poor, a state or a local Ombudsman? The Nebraska experience speaks to these questions.

In previous discussions of the subject, most of which were *a priori* without benefit of empirical data, three reasons were advanced to explain why an Ombudsman would not serve the poor well.[10] First, the poor have special problems not suited to an institution designed to be impartial and conciliatory; the poor need an outspoken advocate. Second, if an Ombudsman somehow manages to correct "little" problems, the larger and more demanding problems will not get the attention their seriousness deserves; as Victor Rosenblum argues, an Ombudsman could "establish the illusion for a lulled populace that all is well because the Ombudsman is on patrol."[11] Third, as a part of the Establishment, the Ombudsman will be suspect, not visible to the poor, and not very accessible.

John Moore has argued persuasively that these objections have been stated much too dogmatically.[12] Data from Nebraska would support Moore's contention that these objections are in some cases premature and in other instances overdrawn. First, data from Nebraska suggest that the kinds of cases brought to the Ombudsman by the poor are similar to his other cases, with the obvious exception of their concern over public welfare administration. In many of the cases, poor Nebraskans did not need the kind of advocate required in a court of law. In the case of justified complaints, the poor got an advocate, as all citizens would, once the Ombudsman decided that the complaint was justified.

Social Reform v. "Little" Problems

What the poor did not get is an advocate who sought fundamental changes in law or administrative policy. This is an especially important absence in the public welfare area. Nebraska law and tradition guarantee local autonomy in the administration of welfare programs. Thus, McNeil was often outside his jurisdiction on welfare cases. Regardless of the complaint's justification, he cannot be an effective advocate in this area. Likewise, many problems the poor face are rooted in law, and, while he can suggest changes in law, the Ombudsman is not as effective here as he is when dealing with administrative procedures or rules.

The second objection spoke of the lulling effect the Ombudsman might produce because he could solve "little" problems. This is an argument that seems to ignore the everyday realities facing the poor. While social reformers continue their (often commendable)

clamor for basic reforms, the simple fact is that the
poor must attempt to cope with their present environment. What is a "little" problem? Is it a missing
welfare check, non-enforcement of housing codes, lack
of a Department of Motor Vehicle licensing office in
poor neighborhoods, or tax forms not printed in Spanish? These are the kinds of problems an Ombudsman can
sometimes address and, although their resolution will
do little toward basic social reforms, the plight of
aggrieved poor citizens may be eased. Responding to
complaints about current procedures and rules does
not necessarily interfere with attention to the larger
issues.

The Nebraska Ombudsman may be suspect by the poor,
as contended in the third objection, but we have no
data to confirm or deny with any certainty. It is obvious, however, that the poor are bringing cases to
his attention. The Ombudsman's caseload from the poor
is in approximate proportion to their number in the
population.

An Ombudsman can help the poor, and Murrell McNeil
has shown that. The important question is how much help
he can provide. On that score, the Nebraska Ombudsman
does not fare so well. To the extent that the Ombudsman
deals with cases from the poor about state taxes, drivers' licenses, and educational benefits for special
students--in other words, cases similar to those coming
from the not-poor--he can be effective. When the poor
raise questions and voice complaints about the welfare
system, he is much less effective. And when the poor
speak about such close-to-home problems as inadequate
street lighting, sub-standard housing, exclusionary
zoning, mistreatment by the police or inadequate police
protection, McNeil is virtually irrelevant. He is not
effective because of a jurisdictional boundary; only
state matters are within his jurisdiction. It then
follows that an Ombudsman at the local level of government in Nebraska would complement McNeil's state level
activities.[13] Neither state nor local Ombudsmen pro-

vide panaceas, but they do seem to constitute one low cost response to complaints that both the poor and the not-poor have about government.

VII

Some Representative Cases

The foregoing caseload analysis provides an introduction to the kind of work the Ombudsman performs. A more complete understanding, however, comes only after exposure to the specifics of some cases. This section presents excerpts from representative cases, masking individual identities, and illustrating several points raised earlier, to demonstrate the many types of cases McNeil receives, and the way in which he operationalizes his statutory jurisdiction.

Examples of Complaints

The first two cases are examples of typical, justified complaints.

> *CASE 1.* The complainant brought to McNeil's attention the allegation that there was not a flagman to direct traffic on a state highway currently under construction. The Department of Road's regulations require all contractors to maintain flagmen for safety reasons. McNeil contacted the Department of Roads to advise them of this complaint. Two days later he received a letter from the department acknowledging the requirement for flagmen and indicating that the contractor would be instructed immediately to provide a flagman on that construction site.

This case is a complaint against both the private contractor for not maintaining proper safety standards and the Department of Roads for not adequately supervising the construction site. The complainant contacted McNeil's office first rather than the Department of Roads. Given the need for quick resolution of this particular problem, it would have been inappropriate for McNeil to suggest that the complainant exhaust other administrative remedies, i.e., the Department of Roads, before he would take the case. This case shows why the Ombudsman, as a practical matter, usually handles a case even if the citizen has not approached the appropriate agency prior to coming to the Ombudsman's office.

> *CASE 2.* Complainant contacted the Ombudsman with the allegation that her city had a very serious sewage problem--in fact, in a creek running adjacent to her property. It was alleged that a broken underground sewer line had not been repaired and, as a consequence, raw sewage was being fed into this creek which in turn led into several larger rivers. Upon receipt of the complaint, the Ombudsman contacted the Department of Environmental Control to inform them of the complaint and request an immediate on-site inspection. The inspection confirmed the allegations. The department was able to persuade the city to immediately effect a temporary remedy and also to agree to finance a more permanent remedy to this problem.

Because the complaint alleged a violation of state laws, despite the fact that inaction by local government had caused the problem, McNeil exercised his jurisdiction and saw to it that the appropriate state agency solved it. This state agency normally has responsibility for the administration of environmentally related laws, so, in fact, the complaint was alleging inaction by a state agency as well as the local entity.

In the preceding case McNeil assumed jurisdiction because a state agency had operating responsibility in the substantive area. This should be contrasted with the following case, which also involves a local government. Here McNeil declined to acknowledge that he had jurisdiction and, therefore, after some minor assistance to the complainant, he dropped his inquiry.

> CASE 3. Complainant alleged that the board members of a small school district were paying themselves salaries in violation of state law, and that, furthermore, the board refused to provide an adequate audit of its various accounts. Upon investigation, the Ombudsman learned that the members of the school board were being compensated for expenses rather than being paid salaries, and that this was perfectly legitimate. State law also provides opportunities for citizens to require an audit of the financial records of local school boards, but the law makes it clear that initiative for this action rests with local citizens and their county attorney.

McNeil concluded that this case was outside his jurisdiction, and he did not pursue the question of an audit. State laws are applicable and McNeil so acknowledged, but the action in question is by a local governmental entity and McNeil does not usually interfere with the actions of local government where some operating responsibilities of a state agency are not involved. He defines his jurisdiction to mean state agencies administering state law, and not the occasional instance where local government is administering state regulations.

Case 4 provides a good example of a complaint judged to be partially justified.

> CASE 4. Complainant said that some land he owned was being condemned by the Department of Roads. After much discussion with the

department, he was convinced the department was offering him a sum significantly less than the land was worth. Furthermore, he alleged that several members of the department told him that there was nothing they wanted to say to the complainant and that if he had any further comments on the matter he ought to go to court. After some initial questions to the Department of Roads, the Ombudsman did not pursue the matter of the complainant's land value any further. The Ombudsman judged this to be a decision properly made by the agency. However, he did pursue the complainant's allegation of unwillingness to communicate by the department. At McNeil's insistence, the appropriate division director in the department agreed to meet with the complainant in one more attempt to resolve their differences.

This case illustrates a partially valid complaint. The Ombudsman did not address himself to the substance of the complaint, namely the amount of compensation for condemned land, but he assured the complainant of a full hearing before appropriate officials in the department.

The following case, also involving the Department of Roads, shows the characteristics of an unjustified complaint. In this case, the Ombudsman played a sympathetic listener to the complainant, but thoroughly agreed with the department's position.

CASE 5. Complainant is an elderly farmer who had a piece of his property condemned and purchased by the Department of Roads for a highway. Complainant alleges that the Department of Roads failed to construct an underpass so that his cattle could be moved from one pasture to another without having to go across the new highway. The Ombudsman's investigation revealed that, during negotiations over purchase of the land by the department, the farmer had declined an offer from the department to share the expense of an underpass. The department did not feel that it had a responsibility to pay for the entire cost of such an underpass because the complainant's cattle had always moved across the old highway when going from one pasture to another and there never had been an underpass. It would still be feasible for the cattle to move across the new highway. The Ombudsman concluded that this complaint was not justified.

Many complaints brought to the Ombudsman fall comletely outside his jurisdiction. Rather than simply indicate his lack of jurisdiction and dismiss the individual, McNeil almost always attempts to provide some assistance to the complainant without making a judgment as to the veracity of the complaint.

CASE 6. Complainant alleged that his local school board did not post in a public place the salaries of all the teachers employed by the board. There apparently is a state law that requires local school boards to post salaries. Complainant had asked the school board to do so, but the board had not, as yet, complied with his request. The Ombudsman lacks jurisdiction in this case primarily because the State Department of Education lacks any jurisdiction, that is, there is no law permitting the State Department of Education to enforce the law about posting salaries; enforcement is a job for the county attorney. Rather than just dismissing the complaint, McNeil wrote a letter to a newly elected member of the school board advising that member of the law, pointing out that there was a complaint that the law had not been followed and suggesting that in the interest of good government she take whatever steps she feels are appropriate.

Informational Inquiries

A large percentage of McNeil's cases are requests for information. Some have complaints imbedded within them, but many are simply straightforward requests for information. For example, one citizen asked about the licensing operation and regulation of salvage yards (auto junk yards) in the state. He was inquiring about this matter so that he would be informed when approaching his local governmental officials about a situation in his city. The Ombudsman wrote to the citizen, sending copies of appropriate state legislation and a suggestion that a specific member of the Department of Roads could answer any further questions.

How the Ombudsman Handles Cases

Personal knowledge. At several points in this report, reference has been made to Murrell McNeil's strong personal knowledge of state law and the operating procedures of state administrative agencies. For the most part, this knowledge is attributable to his previous experience as State Tax Commissioner and Research Analyst for the Legislative Council. Case 7 typifies the kind of response McNeil is qualified to give about a complicated issue.

> CASE 7. Citizen was inquiring about the provisions of the Uniform Budget Act as it pertains to the budgets of Nebraska cities. The question was whether the State Auditor of Public Accounts has the power to veto items in local government budgets, and whether the Uniform Budget Law permits local government to develop surplus or reserve funds. McNeil was able to respond quickly because he helped write the Uniform Budget Act. His response was timely and accurate.

Legislative referrals. Given the large percentage of the total caseload referred to McNeil by legislators, it is important to understand the way McNeil treats these referrals. Because of their obvious importance to the Ombudsman's office, it is conceivable that McNeil would treat senatorial referrals with more deference than other cases. Does McNeil tell complainants referred by senators that they are wrong when, in fact, they are? The case below strengthens an earlier conclusion that the Ombudsman does inform senators when their constituents have presented an unjustified complaint.

> CASE 8. A complainant notified his state senator that there was an almost constant pool of water at one entrance to the driveway of his gasoline station. The complainant maintains that local government has done nothing about it. He stated that because one of the roads at the intersection on which his service station is located is a state highway, the Department of Roads ought to rectify this problem. Upon investigation, the Ombudsman learned that there was a longstanding written agreement between the Department of Roads, the owner of the service station, and the city that the service station owner would make all necessary repairs around the periphery of his property. Furthermore, the Ombudsman learned that, despite the presence of a nearby state highway, the actual spot in question was clearly within the jurisdiction of the city. The Ombudsman informed the senator of his findings and suggested that the complainant was not presenting a valid complaint.

Legislative casework. Nebraska senators do not have much personal staff. When out-of-session, they do not have any staff, and during the sessions, several senators will share the services of one or two clerical personnel. As noted earlier, one consequence of this staffing pattern is a growing tendency for senators, as they gain confidence in McNeil, to ask the Ombudsman for help on matters normally assigned to a legislative staff. Several examples follow:

> CASE 9. A Nebraska senator was asked by one of his constituents about the tax status of church-owned property in Nebraska and also about the legal requirements dealing with the resale of cemetery lots. The senator asked McNeil to provide answers for these questions.

> CASE 10. A state senator asked McNeil to find out what he could about legislation in other states that permits children of prisoners of war or military men missing in action in Vietnam to attend state colleges without paying the normal tuition. After a few letters and phone calls to several places around the country, McNeil was able to gather the relevant information about practices in other states.

> CASE 11. A senator requested information from the Ombudsman about the Department of Motor Vehicles practice of giving individuals with some form of impaired vision driver's licenses. The senator wanted to know what the regulations were and what kinds of restrictions were placed on those whose vision was not 20/20. McNeil learned of the appropriate regulations through a phone call to the Department of Motor Vehicles and so informed the senator in a memorandum.

The three cases are typical of the kinds of information requests that McNeil receives from senators. They can usually be handled by telephone and in a short time. To the extent that such activities for senators detract from McNeil's ability to thoroughly pursue other cases, the senators' requests should be rejected. For the most part, it seems that the senatorial requests for information can usually be handled so quickly that they do not interfere with McNeil's more fundamental work.

There is no question that McNeil's attention to these requests has bolstered his reputation and standing with legislators. They have learned through their many contacts with McNeil that the Ombudsman's office is an appropriate place to seek resolution of constituents' complaints. In other words, the senators use McNeil's office for the traditional Ombudsman role of complaint resolution as well as for help with their personal requests.

Incomplete pursuit. It is inevitable that, in the handling of hundreds of cases, the Ombudsman will occasionally fail to pursue a case to its fullest conclusion. With the benefit of hindsight, it is possible to review McNeil's handling of his caseload and find examples where he could have been more thorough.

>CASE 12. Complainant was a truck driver who was cited for carrying an excess load when he stopped at a roadside weigh station. He alleged that the inspector at the weigh station did not permit him a second weigh at another scale in order to verify the accuracy of the first. This denial was apparently contrary to a "normal" practice followed by roadside inspectors at weigh stations. The complainant was found guilty in county court of carrying an excess load, but, at the time this case was handled, he was appealing that decision. McNeil's response pointed out that McNeil did not have jurisdiction because the matter was still before the courts. Technically, McNeil was correct, but in so stating he failed to perceive and pursue an important distinction apparently being made between state law and administrative practice. All the parties to this dispute, namely, the Ombudsman, the complainant and the Department

of Roads agreed that state law does not allow for a second weigh when the first is in dispute. All parties also agree that it is often the practice of roadside weigh inspectors to permit a second weigh when so requested. McNeil's failure to pursue this gap between law and practice and at least provide a reasonable criterion for the exercise of discretion by roadside inspectors prevented a resolution that would head off future complaints.

CASE 13. Complainant alleged that he was denied the opportunity to take a merit-system examination for a state position on the grounds that he did not have either previous work experience or appropriate college course work. Complainant acknowledged the lack of previous work experience but insisted that he has appropriate college course work and that his official university transcript does not so indicate because he took the course work in university departments not usually associated with this type of work. Upon investigation, the Ombudsman verified the appropriateness of the job description and agreed with the agency that the individual did not meet the job specification as it stood, and therefore he was not entitled to take the examination for the position. What the Ombudsman apparently failed to do, as did the agency, was to investigate the exact nature of the course work that the complainant claimed was appropriate. Such investigation may have revealed that the course work was appropriate despite what seemed to be inappropriate course titles.

It is surmised that the Ombudsman's investigation into the above cases left something to be desired. However, there is no suggestion that this type of incomplete action was typical. On the contrary, these few cases are clearly exceptions, and stand out for that reason.

Coordination. At several points the Ombudsman has had the opportunity to coordinate the actions of several agencies and officials in an attempt to resolve complicated issues that cross jurisdictional lines. In these cases, as a result of his efforts, several entangled and complicated issues were clarified. For instance:

> CASE 14. The residents of a small Nebraska town that bordered on Kansas pointed out that the closest and most convenient mental health center was in Kansas. Nebraska state law, however, does not permit reimbursement by the state for such treatment at out-of-state clinics. After discussion with several agency personnel and the state senator from the area, McNeil was able to secure agreement that it was reasonable for these Nebraskans to seek help in Kansas and to be reimbursed where appropriate. Through McNeil's efforts the senator has expressed agreement to introduce legislation permitting reimbursement in this case.

Complexity and thoroughness. The last case to be presented is an example of McNeil's persistence and ability to pursue complicated issues, sometimes over several months, to appropriate conclusions. Whether the complaint is ultimately judged justifiable or not, the Ombudsman's thoroughness is impressive.

> CASE 15. A complaint was brought to the Ombudsman's attention by a legal aid society on behalf of a woman who had her ADC monthly check stolen, her signature forged, and the check cashed. The complainant submitted forms for the issuance of a duplicate state warrant but then ran into several problems and still had not received a duplicate warrant three months later. The legal aid office alleged that there were many such requests for duplicate warrants which were being held up some-

where in the bureaucratic process. The delays worked an unfair hardship on the citizens affected. The Ombudsman was forced to deal with the three state agencies which are involved in the issuance of welfare payments and duplicate warrants: Office of the State Treasurer, Department of Administrative Services, and Department of Welfare. Each office had an explanation for the delay in the issuance of duplicate warrants that generally exonerated itself and placed responsibility with either one of the other two state agencies or the local welfare office. It was in this context that the Ombudsman pursued this case and recommended several important administrative changes. For instance, as a result of his investigation, each agency will now date-stamp all requests for replacement forms so that it will be easier in the future to identify any source of delay in the process required to issue warrants. Another important issue was the State Treasurer's alleged refusal to pay for duplicate checks or warrants which had been originally cashed with a forged signature and then paid by the State Treasurer. The result of this action was to deprive the legitimate recipient of a stolen welfare check from ever receiving the appropriate money. The Ombudsman suggested that recourse was available to the Treasurer from the bank which honored the forged signature. As a result of McNeil's efforts, well over 100 requests for duplicate warrants which had been delayed for many months were finally honored.

This case serves also to illustrate a partial exception to the previous conclusion that the Ombudsman is not very effective in welfare-related cases. The conclusion still holds because most welfare-related problems, as noted earlier, deal with discretionary judgments by county welfare officials, who are outside the jurisdiction of the Ombudsman. However, in a case in which a welfare issue clearly involves state agencies, McNeil had jurisdiction and proved an effective spokesman for the aggrieved citizen. Not only was the citizen who initially brought the complaint satisfied, but as a consequence of McNeil's efforts a more general policy was established that appears to offer good probability of expediting and making fairer the distribution of duplicate warrants for stolen or lost welfare checks.

VIII

External Relationships: The Political and Administrative Environment

Independence

The legislation that established Nebraska's Ombudsman closely followed Walter Gellhorn's model statute,[1] which, in turn, was inspired by the traditional Scandinavian office. Ensuring the Ombudsman's independence is an important goal of the legislation. His legal independence stems from the provisions of the bill which (1) call for appointment to a long term with a fixed salary; (2) provide for removal from office only by an extraordinary legislative majority if he has been "guilty of neglect of duty or misconduct;" and (3) grant immunity from judicial review of his opinions or actions as Ombudsman. These legal attributes give the Ombudsman potential independence of action but they do not guarantee it.

Several roadblocks to successful performance of the Ombudsman's responsibilities are possible; and the Nebraska Ombudsman (or any Ombudsman) must recognize them. He must realize that he is not completely free to perform as he chooses; he has constituents in the political/administrative arena who must be satisfied or, to varying degrees, they may make life difficult for him. Noting some of the problems that can be created for the Ombudsman should highlight his dependence upon the support of others.[2] To the extent that the Ombudsman cannot ignore these realities, he is not truly independent.

85

Potential Checks on Independence

Funding. The Nebraska Ombudsman's office was established by a one-vote margin in the Unicameral, as we have seen, and it was funded initially by the federal government with only a pittance from state government. McNeil operated from May 1971 to June 1973 without a state-appropriated budget. Naturally, he was concerned that when the federal grant expired, the state legislature might not take over the funding. Furthermore, because the governor is deeply involved in budget preparation and appropriation, there was the possibility of gubernatorial displeasure being voiced at budget time. In fact, the legislature and the governor did agree to fund the office, but their support was never a certainty in advance.

Now that McNeil has cleared the hurdle of that first state appropriation, succeeding years should be easier in the sense that the office's survival probably will not be at issue, although the amount of funding will be. Can the Ombudsman continue to function with the bare bones staffing he now has? If McNeil wants to increase his staff, as an example of an expenditure increase, he will need approval from the legislature and the governor.

Legislative revision. LB 521, like any other state law, can be altered. Unhappiness with the Ombudsman's performance could lead to legislative changes. For instance, if a senator felt that McNeil was being too harsh or too demanding of a particular agency, he could introduce legislation to remove that agency from McNeil's jurisdiction. It is important to remember that the entire office could be abolished by the legislature with or without the governor's concurrence; the Ombudsman is not written into the Constitution. Regardless of whether such an attempt would succeed, the possibility of senatorial displeasure being reflected in new legislation is real. As such, it must, in some way, affect the Ombudsman.

Lack of gubernatorial cooperation. It is conceivable that the governor could direct his department heads not to cooperate with the Ombudsman. The lack of cooperation could result in difficulties for the Ombudsman when he sought information from an agency. At the extreme, it could force the Ombudsman to use his subpoena power, a cumbersome weapon that represents an all-out clash between the Ombudsman and an agency. Nebraska's Governor has chosen to cooperate with the Ombudsman in every way he can, but there is no guarantee of continued good will, especially with a new governor.

Lack of agency cooperation. Despite avowed gubernatorial cooperation, the Ombudsman must still rely upon agency personnel, some of whom are not responsible to the governor, for assistance in his casework. An Ombudsman office can be efficient only if it receives agency help. If one goal of the Ombudsman is a speedy reply to the citizen, he would be blocked by delayed responses from the agency.

Ombudsman's Reaction

The point of this discussion is that the Ombudsman has constituents in the political and administrative aspects of government that he cannot ignore. To the extent that he takes these constituents into account, he is no longer the completely independent official often mentioned in discussions of the Ombudsman institution. Every Ombudsman responds to his constituents in a different way; McNeil's style has been characterized by caution.

McNeil is careful not to step outside his legislatively mandated jurisdiction. When he receives a case dealing with a local government, for example, he makes clear to both citizen and relevant local official his lack of official jurisdiction. Whatever assistance he provides is informal and strictly in the interest of helping resolve conflicts.

Expenditures by the Ombudsman's office have been modest. McNeil has been sensitive to the need for low-cost operation in order to win senatorial favor. Because salaries are such a large percentage of total expenditures, McNeil has not hired a full-time professional staff member to assist him. Likewise, as we have seen, cost was one important consideration in his decision not to open an office in Omaha.

Mindful of the need for agency cooperation, McNeil has used his access to the mass media to publicize his office but not to single out agency errors. One of his operating rules is not to mention agencies by name in either his contacts with the media or his annual reports. The drawback to this policy is that it forces his public commentary into the abstract. The advantage stems from an agency's knowledge that full cooperation with the Ombudsman will never cause it embarrassment in the press.

As a last illustration of McNeil's cautious style, we should again mention his willingness to perform tasks for the senators that normally fall outside an Ombudsman's purview. It simply does not make sense for McNeil to refuse these possibly "improper" requests if he wants to maintain the close personal rapport he enjoys with most legislators. His attention to his legislative constituency has paid dividends in their willingness to support him. The price McNeil has paid is primarily in terms of time. The trade-off of time for support was certainly worthwhile during the first years of the office. Now that the first phase of development is over and the Ombudsman is an established innovation in Nebraska government, the value of the trade-off is less apparent.

Evaluations by Political and Administrative Constituents

Through observations, personal interviews, and mail questionnaires, data have been gathered that document the favorable impression of McNeil's efforts held by the governor, legislators, and state administrators. It is a remarkable accomplishment to have achieved McNeil's level of support in all these constituencies.

Gubernatorial support. The best indicator of McNeil's support from the governor came at budget time during the 1973 legislative session; the governor backed McNeil's budget request. There are additional signs of favorable gubernatorial evaluation. Several members of the governor's staff mentioned privately that they were pleased with McNeil's presence and the way he handled the job. Many issues that would otherwise appear in the press are handled in the Ombudsman's office. By resolving citizens' complaints, the Ombudsman can prevent some embarrassment for the administration when an agency has erred. This characteristic, combined with McNeil's unwillingness to mention specific agencies in his public commentary, means that the Ombudsman can be politically helpful to the governor simply through the performance of his job.

Awareness of the potential political advantages plus a desire to run an efficient administration prompted Governor Exon to cooperate fully with McNeil right from the first. McNeil was invited to a meeting of department heads soon after taking office in 1971. At this meeting, the governor told those present that he expected them to assist and not hinder McNeil's efforts. McNeil continues to meet monthly with representatives of the major departments.

Legislative support and evaluation. McNeil is widely respected among senators as a competent man who can be trusted; his reputation is above question. Starting with this reputation and following it by providing quick and usually thorough resolution of the cases senators refer, McNeil has been able to maintain their confidence. An important test of McNeil's legislative acceptance came during his budget request, and, as already mentioned, the legislature passed his budget without change.

McNeil works hard at legislative relations. Three examples will show how sensitive he is to the need for senatorial approval: (1) Whenever McNeil writes a letter to a citizen who has been referred by a senator, the letter starts with "Senator ___ asked me to look into..." and ends with "Senator ___ and I thank you for the chance to help." (and a carbon copy is sent to the senator). (2) When McNeil's investigation reveals the need for new or amended legislation, he will write a memo to appropriate senators. This courtesy keeps senators informed in areas of concern to them. (3) At the beginning of the 1973 legislative session, 11 newly elected senators (22 percent of the legislature) were on the floor.

Not one to wait long in the wings, McNeil took the initiative and invited the newcomers to a meeting, where he briefed them about his office. The advantage of the meeting became apparent as the freshman senators started referring cases to McNeil. These efforts are typical of McNeil's political skills.

McNeil's attention to legislators has paid handsome non-pecuniary dividends. As Table 11 indicates, legislators are pleased with McNeil's performance. Perhaps one reason for their favorable impression stems from their perception that the Ombudsman has encouraged at least some improvement within the administrative agencies. This was one of the office's chief virtues as originally suggested by Senator Schmit during the legislative history of LB 521. Although legislators' perceptions about McNeil's impact on agencies are not firm and irrefutable evidence of such impact, these perceptions play an important role in McNeil's legislative support.

An Ombudsman may have a direct impact upon state law by suggesting and arguing for changes in the law. Some Ombudsmen formally publish their recommendations for changes in law as part of their annual reports. They also appear before legislative committees to argue their cause. The Nebraska Ombudsman has chosen not to follow that route. Instead, he relies upon a more informal procedure in which he calls inequities or objectionable circumstances in law to the attention of specific legislators who are interested in that policy area. There is no reason to doubt the effectiveness of the informal approach, and there are several known instances when McNeil has recommended a change and received immediate favorable reaction from the legislature.

Administrative relations. McNeil understands, and empathizes with the individuals who staff the agencies. These feelings cause McNeil to approach agencies with openness and willingness to cooperate rather than with a desire for battle with an adversary. His style, backed by his reputation, accounts for the good relations he maintains with administrators.

So far, McNeil has not used his subpoena power in the course of an investigation. Only once has he threatened to use it, and in that instance, the requested information was soon on his desk.

An indication of his relationship with administrators comes from the questionnaire sent to a sample of middle and top level state administrators.[3] (There were 156 responses.) At the most basic level, almost all of the respondents knew that Nebraska has an Ombudsman (96 percent) and a substantial majority were able to correctly identify his functions (61 percent, using strict coding criteria). Furthermore, 54.5 percent of the respondents acknowledged knowing Murrell McNeil personally. Responses were not just based on acquaintance with McNeil; most of them had dealt with him in the course of business: 63 percent indicated at least one contact with the Ombudsman's office about a complaint or question. By indicating at least four business contacts with the Ombudsman, one-third of the sample showed frequent interaction with McNeil.

The data show that when the sample was asked a series of evaluation questions, they were responding out of an awareness of the new state Ombudsman and his functions. On the whole, respondents had a positive impression of the Ombudsman. To the question "What general impression have you gained of the Ombudsman?", they answered with the following distribution:

Very positive	64.7%
Somewhat positive	19.9
Somewhat negative	1.3
Very negative	0.0
Uncertain	11.5
No response	2.6
	100 % (156)

Two interesting trends emerged upon further analysis. First, the respondents who had worked longer in state government were more favorable in their impressions: administrators with 11 to 20 years of state government service were more favorably impressed than those with 10 or fewer years of service.[4] Second, those respondents who personally knew McNeil were more inclined to rate him positively than those who did not know him. As it turns out, the administrators who have been in state government longer also are more likely to know the Ombudsman personally, so the relationships are interesting but probably not independent of each other. What is important, however, is to note again the way in which McNeil's personal reputation plays a part in administrators' perceptions and evaluations.

Impact of the Ombudsman. Table 12 shows the responses to three related questions. The slight drop-off of positive responses between questions 1 and 2 is probably the consequence of some Nebraska pride--the idea is good, but for a few administrators, Nebraska doesn't need one. The strong response in question 3 that the Ombudsman should become a permanent part of state government is dramatic evidence of McNeil's acceptance. Again, more of those with 11 to 20 years of state employment saw a need for an Ombudsman in Nebraska and felt the office should be permanent than those who had worked 10 years or less.

In Table 12, an apparent unwillingness to admit the Ombudsman had an impact on their own department's policies is juxtaposed with perceptions about the Ombudsman's impact on state government. Approximately two-thirds of the respondents perceive at least some impact by the Ombudsman in the administration of state laws. Again, those with lengthier government service and those who knew McNeil personally were more inclined to perceive at least some impact by the Ombudsman.

Participation with a legislative study committee. There are two additional pieces of information that point to the impact McNeil is having on the bureaucracy. They both fall into the category of "preventive medicine." During the interim between sessions, the Unicameral creates a Study Committee on Rules and Regulations. This committee systematically reviews regulations by which agencies implement state law, and it specifically seeks assurance that administrative rules and regulations do not conflict with or change the meaning of a law. In 1973, Murrell McNeil was invited to sit with the committee as it discussed the rules and regulations of the agencies under scrutiny. In this manner, the Ombudsman can offer his judgment about the presence of any unfair, arbitrary, or otherwise objectionable administrative rule. His judgment may have been informed by a specific case or simply result from his general experience. Either way, his participation in the committee's work can head off future citizen complaints.

Another form of preventive medicine in which McNeil has been involved has been initiated by several administrators. McNeil reports that recently a few administrators have informed him that their agency had just made a mistake and McNeil would undoubtedly hear about it from aggrieved citizens. This demonstrates that McNeil is taken seriously by these bureaucrats, and it is a compliment to the agency personnel that they are conscientious enough to admit a mistake. This advance notice by administrators also gives them an early opportunity to explain their side of the problem to McNeil.

Summary

While legislators and administrators share similar (and favorable) attitudes about the Ombudsman, data from the legislators show a more positive attitude about McNeil's work and his impact on state agencies than the data from administrators. Given a choice, an Ombudsman should be pleased with the legislative skewing of the data. In the final analysis, legislators foot the bill.

Although our simple questionnaires cannot discover it, there is probably a strong relationship between the legislative and administrative data sets. Positive legislative attitudes will have an important spin-off onto administrative attitudes. Someone who has McNeil's clear-cut legislative support, plus his strong personal reputation, is hard for astute administrators to ignore. In a practical sense, McNeil's strong legislative backing makes administrative acceptance of his suggestions and recommendations more likely.

More than anything else, this chapter has painted a more dramatically successful image of the office than might have been expected before McNeil's appointment. A comparison of the small margin by which LB 521 became law, and the uncertain future that awaited the bill at the hands of the Executive Board, with the attitudes expressed now by the governor, legislators, and administrators provides a startling contrast.

Summary of Evaluations

The consequences of any public service are difficult to measure, especially if an intangible "product" is the output. If a road department builds a highway, the impact of that highway is more easily ascertained than if the governmental output being measured is an improved public administration or greater citizen satisfaction with government. The latter two outputs are among those that should be used to measure the Ombudsman's impact.

As an Ombudsman seeks improvement in the administration of laws, he addresses three problems of bureaucracy in James Q. Wilson's formulation: equity, responsiveness, and efficiency.[1] Equity refers to the need for like cases to be treated alike, while responsiveness appeals to the contrary need for comparison, exceptions and awareness of mitigating circumstances as a part of administration decisionmaking. The efficiency problem deals with the need to "maximize output for a given expenditure, or minimizing expenditures for a given output."[2] Finding the right blend of these three values--equity, responsiveness, and efficiency--constitutes the basic responsibility of an Ombudsman. Not an easy task, nor is it easy for an observer to measure success and failure.

As some of the cases cited in Chapter VII illustrate, and a reading of the complete case file substantiates, McNeil has insisted upon correction where it is clear that a citizen is not being treated equitably.

95

McNeil has been particularly concerned that the special circumstances surrounding a case are taken into account. A search for equity and responsiveness has guided the Ombudsman.

One of McNeil's chief contributions to administrative efficiency has been his repeated demonstration to agencies of the value of careful, thorough documentation of a case. The documentation, he has argued, must be coupled with a complete explanation to the citizen. Lack of communication or inadequate communication from agencies to citizens is frequently the underlying cause of citizens' complaints.

In the long run, an increasing amount of equity, responsiveness, and efficiency in administrative decisionmaking will produce an increase in citizen satisfaction with government. Again, citizen satisfaction is difficult to measure. Given the unavailability of funds to conduct a sample survey of Nebraska citizens, and our unwillingness to imperil the Ombudsman's public trust by directly interviewing his clientele, we have only sketchy evidence, at best, of the impact McNeil has had on the public.

One piece of evidence is a small survey McNeil conducted. On two different occasions, he sent approximately 100 postcards to citizens whose cases were closed during the preceding two months. One batch of postcards indicated that the citizen's signature was needed, while the other batch was to be anonymous (although several people volunarily signed their names). Nearly 90 percent of the respondents to both batches of postcards indicated their satisfaction with the office (the return rate was approximately 60 percent). The high satisfaction rate was present in the face of a significant number of cases in which citizens were told that their complaint was unjustified.

McNeil has clearly had some impact and has moved Nebraska government closer to the goals of equity, responsiveness, and efficiency. Before trying to offer some summary evaluation of his contribution, a few suggestions for improvement will be mentioned.

Recommendations

Suggestions for the Ombudsman's consideration have been offered at several points in this report. For emphasis, they are collected and reiterated below.

Staff increase. For two years, Murrell McNeil has personally handled the entire caseload. While this policy was understandable under the circumstances, the Ombudsman's full potential cannot be reached without an expansion in his staff. Adding at least one professional staff member would provide McNeil with the time he needs for three vital functions.

First, by assigning other staff to handle the more routine cases, McNeil would become more available for the time-consuming, complicated, and/or sensitive cases. During the second year of operation, there has been a marked increase in the number of complicated cases, many of them involving serious accusations of impropriety by state agency personnel. As time passes and the Ombudsman becomes even more visible and accepted, this trend is likely to increase. A thorough job on this type of case demands a time commitment that McNeil will find increasingly difficult to allocate unless additional staff help is available.

Second, additional staff would allow McNeil time for own-motion investigations. In the pursuit of information about specific cases, the Ombudsman has occasionally discovered administrative policies or procedures that could stand improvement. Lack of time has been one of the chief reasons that McNeil did not pursue the matter further after the case at hand had been resolved. Furthermore, someone with McNeil's experience and perception knows of dubious situations that may not have been the subject of a specific complaint. His statutory power to investigate on his own motion should be implemented.

Third, additional staff would permit time for generating more publicity. The need for publicity is virtually endless, and Nebraska's geography makes it a time-consuming venture. The Ombudsman's publicity needs vary and he should now be more discriminating in such use of his time. For instance, time spent in publicity efforts in Lincoln could probably be better spent in Omaha. Lincoln residents seem aware of McNeil's activities, through coverage in the media and because it is the capital city. Omaha residents, however, have contributed less than their proportionate share of cases and more attention to publicity in Omaha would seem appropriate. For example, joint speaking engagements with Omaha senators could publicize the office while not appearing to infringe upon the senators' home turf.

The primary value of additional staff is the time it would provide for the Ombudsman to do some of the non-routine casework. For comparative purposes, it is worth noting that the Nebraska office has a smaller staff than any other Ombudsman office in the country. Hawaii, Iowa, and Seattle all have larger staffs and yet they serve populations of approximately similar size.

Keeping records and utilizing files. The quality of records kept by the office is high. Murrell McNeil is well aware of the importance of a good record keeping system. However, the office's excellent organizational memory has not been used to its fullest advantage. After two years of experience, the files now contain ample data for trend analysis; e.g., has the passage of law x produced more complaints about its administration than the complaints registered against the administration of the law it replaced? The excellent filing system could also be used to greater advantage in the preparation of the Ombudsman's annual reports. These reports have not contained examples of cases handled during the preceding year. A more thorough understanding of his activities could be achieved if McNeil would utilize his files to provide examples of his work.

Legislative inquiries. Referral of cases from senators should be a welcome addition to the Ombudsman's caseload. However, the tendency for senators to ask McNeil questions more properly addressed to legislative staff presents a potential problem. So far, the demands placed on McNeil's time by these inquiries have not been burdensome. The danger rests in creating the habit. As senators get accustomed to this service from McNeil, they will use him for this purpose at an increasing rate, unless and until they bolster their own meager staff assistance. The Ombudsman should find a way to reduce the number of requests for information from senators.

Jurisdiction. From the number of complaints McNeil has received about local government, it is apparent that Nebraskans have grievances against their local governments. Local government is clearly outside McNeil's jurisdiction. A careful look at the experience of the Hawaii and Iowa Ombudsmen in handling local government cases might provide McNeil some guidance on the matter. It is not inconceivable that, at a future date, McNeil might be inclined to recommend an expansion of his jurisdiction. The situation bears watching.

Completeness of investigation. A small percentage of cases could have been pursued further. In some instances, there are reasons why the investigation stopped before reaching a more thorough conclusion. On the other hand, careful attention must be paid to each case so that all ramifications are explored; as the number of completed cases increases additional staff is needed to insure thoroughness.

Lessons from the Nebraska Innovation

Implicit in many of the comments found in previous chapters is the belief that what happened in Nebraska contains some lessons for other governmental jurisdictions, both state and local. Naturally, any generalizations from this single case must be made carefully; yet, we have so little actual experience in this country with classical Ombudsmen that despite our caution about over-generalization, a recapitulation seems appropriate of the main points to be learned from the Nebraska Ombudsman's experience. The following comments are organized to correspond to the topics covered in the preceding chapters.

The politics of adoption. As with most legislation, passage of the Ombudsman enabling legislation requires the firm commitment of at least one skillful legislator who is respected by his colleagues and has many friends within the legislature. Commitment is the key: because of its innovative character this kind of bill cannot be pushed half-heartedly if it is going to pass. When the bill is being considered in committee and on the floor, the author(s) must be prepared to compromise and disarm critics. Thus in Nebraska Senator Schmit ran into criticism over the amount of the Ombudsman's salary, so he simply agreed to remove the specific dollar amount from the bill and authorize the Executive Board to set the salary. Another compromise occurred when one senator objected to the wording in the original bill that would have guaranteed privileged communication to the Ombudsman from inmates in all state institutions. The offending section was removed.

Compromise will obviously be essential in implementing this innovation. How far the compromise should be permitted to carry the sponsors away from the original version is simply impossible to say in an *a priori* fashion.

In the course of legislative consideration, the attitudes created among legislators about the functions and responsibilities of the new office will have a lasting impact on the Ombudsman's operations. Proponents of the legislation must be careful not to create false hopes or expectations that could come back to haunt the Ombudsman later. After all, an Ombudsman is not a knight on a white horse who is out to slay the bureaucratic dragon. Some tempering of enthusiasm at this stage will help later.

If the Ombudsman bill doesn't originate with the governor or have his early support then the governor must be persuaded that it is to his advantage--or at least not to his disadvantage--to have an Ombudsman. Appealing to the governor's political instincts, Ombudsman proponents can argue that there are at least two reasons why the governor should sign the bill: (1) By approving the idea, the governor can associate himself with an important "good government" reform that will "make government more responsive to the people;" and (2) by approving the idea, the governor can help establish an office which will serve the purpose of relatively quiet complaint resolution and, therefore, many issues that might end up in the press and offer some embarrassment will be resolved in-house.

If any Ombudsman legislation is to pass, the media must not be hostile. In Nebraska the press did not comment much during debate on the bill, but what did appear was either favorable or straightforward news reporting of the situation. The press served a useful role in prodding the Executive Board to stop delaying the nomination. Proponents of Ombudsman legislation would be well advised to keep the media fully informed of their intentions and generate as much publicity as possible for their actions; attempts to influence editorial policy by making presentations to editors, publishers and station managers would also seem desirable.

Good press relations will always be important to the Ombudsman. To facilitate good relations the Ombudsman might want to take the initiative and seek out the media. He can suggest that they do stories on the office and run interviews with him. During his contact with the media the Ombudsman must maintain the confidentiality of his case records and not succumb to the almost inevitable requests to discuss specific cases in all their detail.

Appointing an acceptable and capable Ombudsman. Murrell McNeil's success suggests that it may be beneficial to appoint a person who is from the jurisdiction, rather than an "outsider." Not only should the Ombudsman be someone who has experience in administration and bureaucratic politics, but additionally he should have the respect of both politicians and bureaucrats--not be universally loved, but respected. And to prevent suspicions that could undermine this respect an Ombudsman must be someone who will not be perceived by others as being politically motivated or planning a political career. In practice this probably requires appointment of someone who has already established a bureaucratic career, or an active or retired judge, or someone whose reputation for good government and non-partisan issue involvement places him above politically motivated suspicion.

Most importantly, an Ombudsman must be a good listener. Effective listening is an art, and the job specifications for an Ombudsman demand a person who has the patience and sensitivity to afford every complainant a fair hearing. It would be the height of folly to appoint a person whose previous experience and reputation for integrity match the formal job specifications, but who does not fully appreciate the demands of a job that requires constant, intimate public contact on a daily basis.

Relations with other complaint offices. In most cases an Ombudsman will be established in jurisdictions that already have some other forms of complaint handling. The Ombudsman will develop a *modus vivendi* with them. In fact, it may be good political strategy during the consideration of the legislation to discuss openly the relationship that should develop between the various complaint offices in the jurisdiction. One conclusion seems clear--the Ombudsman should not attempt to take over all complaint handling functions.

Office staffing and operation. The size of the Ombudsman'a budget will be a crucial and controversial issue. During debate the projected budget and number of office personnel should be articulated so that the Ombudsman, after appointment, will have a reasonable awareness of legislative intent. Practically speaking, there is no way this topic (budget and staff) can be kept out of legislative consideration. Accordingly the matter should be approached openly. To do otherwise, and perhaps seriously underestimate the office's requirements, would risk placing the Ombudsman in a compromised position and possibly injuring his reputation with legislators. While there is a real and understandable need to keep the office and its budget relatively small, the sponsors of Ombudsman legislation and the new Ombudsman must make it clear that an effective Ombudsman needs staff. Personnel salaries account for the single largest percentage of the office budget.

Although the Ombudsman cannot be a one-man show for too long, he should plan to handle most, if not all, of the initial caseload. He will then know the exact nature of the caseload and this knowledge will be helpful in deciding upon the kind of background he needs in other staff members. His fulltime attention to the caseload initially will also permit the development of a personal relationship with the relevant administrative agency staff.

An accurate and comprehensive record keeping system is essential for the development of an organizational memory. More than most government offices, that of an Ombudsman has a special obligation to be efficient in its paperwork. Lost or misfiled papers, delay in response, inability to reconstruct past events, and similar bureaucratic snafus are simply not to be tolerated from an Ombudsman. One of the factors helping produce a strong positive evaluation of McNeil's operations is his office's thorough and systematic records.

Data in previous chapters show the large number of non-complaint cases McNeil handles. This open-door policy produces a clear demand on staff time; inquiries take time to answer. Yet, it is difficult for an Ombudsman, especially a new one, to refuse inquiries and no-jurisdiction cases. If the demands of non-complaint cases become too burdensome, perhaps the Ombudsman could

recommend the establishment of an information office--
such as the one in Hawaii--to help divert inquiries
from this office.

Caseload jurisdiction. In approximately one-third
of the Nebraska Ombudsman's total caseload he is dealing
with matters outside his statutorily defined jurisdiction. The largest single category of these no-jurisdiction cases, about 38 percent, involve local government.
Several propositions follow from this single fact.
First, there is an obvious need for continuous publicity
which stresses the office's jurisdiction. Second, Nebraskans apparently find many occasions to complain
about their local government. Third, the Nebraska Ombudsman is moving toward a difficult situation, in which
the number of local government complaints could increase
further. This will probably occur because complainants
with local government problems, who are informally assisted by McNeil in accordance with his open-door policy,
will not only continue to use McNeil but will also encourage other citizens to follow the same route.

Options for local governments. To the extent that
the local government cases require a significant amount
of staff time they represent a deviation from the office's original goal of improving the quality of state
government administration. At that point the Ombudsman
might wish to recommend one of several alternative responses. The Ombudsman's jurisdiction could be extended
to include all local government; or the state could
establish regional, multi-county Ombudsmen, either independent of or working under direction of the state
Ombudsman; or the state could require (or offer strong
inducements for) each county and major city to establish an Ombudsman. The poor would be primary beneficiaries, although surely not the only ones, of any extension of the state Ombudsman's jurisdiction into local
government, or state mandating or encouragement of local
establishment of Ombudsman offices. This would automatically provide a grievance official who has the jurisdiction to deal with many of the problems that the poor
face.

Giving the state Ombudsman jurisdiction over all local government affairs could lead to more problems than it would solve. The administrative apparatus required for a broadening of jurisdiction--especially in a geographically large state--would be so extensive that it would likely result in a bureaucracy beset with many of the problems it was addressing in other agencies. An Ombudsman's office must be small, afford personalized attention to each case, and avoid at all costs the need for elaborate inter-office communication patterns and authority relations. Speaking practically, the major stumbling block to an extension of state authority or a forced implementation of an Ombudsman plan under state orders is the strong belief in localism and home rule. Nebraskans, and for that matter citizens in most states, adhere to the myth that local government is their government, and because it is "close" to them they don't easily accept state "interference" in the way they run their business. It would probably be impossible to get far with legislation that required a local Ombudsman.

The most promising avenue for those who see both the need to relieve the state Ombudsman of local grievances and the need for a locally based complaint resolution office would seem to point toward the use of state money as an inducement. Under this scheme, the state would offer to fund all or a large percentage of the operating costs for the first few years of a local Ombudsman office. Naturally, the state would insist upon certain conditions--perhaps adoption of an ordinance similar in intent to the state Ombudsman legislation. In other words, the state would perform the same role for its local governments as the federal government did when it funded the Nebraska Ombudsman.

Relations with legislators. If there is one single theme to be discerned from the Nebraska Ombudsman's experience it is the importance of maintaining good relations with legislators. As the body to whom the Ombudsman is ultimately responsible, and that also provides funds for the office, the legislature is an important constituent. Contrary to the impressions generated from a reading of some earlier literature on Ombudsmen, no Ombudsman is so independent that he can safely ignore such constituents.[3] Thus an Ombudsman cannot ignore legislators under the guise of seeking independence. Rather, an Ombudsman should work closely with legislators and keep them thoroughly informed about his activities. A key test of an Ombudsman's real independence occurs when he feels the need, after investigation of the specific details of a case, to tell a legislator that his constituent is wrong. As long as an Ombudsman can say "No" to a legislator or his constituent when the facts merit a negative answer, the Ombudsman is, in fact, independent. By building respect for himself and his office, an Ombudsman should be able to say "No" in specific cases and still maintain the legislators' general support for the office.

Some Concluding Observations

During floor debate on LB 521, four objections were raised: it was too new an idea, it would cost too much, it would hamper administrators, and legislators were Ombudsmen already. With the exception of the first objection, which is undercut by McNeil's success, McNeil has carefully and skillfully addressed himself to the objections. He has kept costs down to approximately the estimate Senator Schmit offered during debate, and that is a modest expenditure. In his attempt to keep expenditures down, McNeil has been aided by a caseload that has been manageable for a hard working small staff. McNeil has made every effort not to hamper administrators or create unnecessary paperwork for them. He does this not only in response to the objection, but as a result of his many years as an administrator. Administrators have a high regard for him, and McNeil has apparently shown legislators that his function as an Ombudsman does not deprive them of their traditional relationships with their constituents.

It should be apparent by now that the attempted Nebraska innovation has been successful. In the most basic sense, it has been successful because it has survived. The survival threshold was formally crossed when the state agreed to fund the office. Until that point, the Ombudsman's activities had cost the state hardly any money; allocation of funds is a key indicator of health for any public entity.

The Ombudsman has done much more than merely survive the first two years. He has had a significant and positive impact on hundreds of Nebraskans whose complaints were resolved and whose inquiries were answered. Even those citizens who brought forward complaints judged to be unjustified were aided by an impartial hearing of their cases. Administrators and legislators agree that McNeil has had an impact on administrative agencies.[4]

Murrell McNeil is a cautious man. He has fulfilled his responsibilities in a conscientious and thoroughly professional manner. His contribution to Nebraska government could be heightened by a slightly more aggressive stance toward the agencies. Tactics such as own-motion investigations, public mention of specific agencies in reference to particular cases, and more extensive publicity efforts in Omaha will make the Ombudsman even more effective and probably enhance his public reputation.

NOTES

Notes to Chapter I

[1] See Donald C. Rowat, "The Spread of the Ombudsman Idea" in Stanley V. Anderson, ed., *Ombudsmen for American Government?* (Englewood Cliffs: Prentice-Hall, 1968), pp. 7-36. In the short time since Rowat wrote this chapter, many new jurisdictions have been added to the list. For a more current listing see Kent M. Weeks, *Ombudsmen Around the World: A Comparative Chart* (Berkeley: Institute of Governmental Studies, University of California, 1973).

[2] For a more elaborate discussion of defining characteristics, see Anderson, *op. cit.*, especially Chapters II and V and the model statute in the Appendix. For common variations on the original version, see the essays in Alan J. Wyner, ed., *Executive Ombudsmen in the United States* (Berkeley: Institute of Governmental Studies, University of California, 1973).

[3] Stanley V. Anderson, *Ombudsman Papers: American Experience and Proposals* (Berkeley: Institute of Governmental Studies, University of California, 1969), p. 3.

[4] The Dayton, Ohio Ombudsman bears many similarities to the classical version but it is not included here because it is not based on a statute but rather on the voluntary acquiescence of the city, county and school board. For more see Leonard D. Goodstein, *An Evaluation of the Dayton Ombudsman* (Dayton: Charles F. Kettering Foundation, 1972).

[5] For more on executive Ombudsmen see Wyner, *op. cit.*, especially pp. 305-315.

Notes to Chapter I cont'd.

[6] E. Terry Sanford, *Storm Over the States* (New York: McGraw-Hill, 1967), esp. Ch. I. Mr. Justice Louis Brandeis called the states "laboratories for democracy." See *New State Ice Co. v. Liebmann* 285 U.S. 262 (1932).

[7] For a concise but accurate listing of some prominent examples of innovations by state governments see Walter W. Heller, *New Dimensions of Political Economy* (New York: W. W. Norton, 1967), esp. pp. 124-25. On this same point, also see Ira Sharkansky, *The Maligned States* (New York: McGraw-Hill, 1972).

[8] Mohr, "Determinants of Innovation in Organizations," *American Political Science Review,* 63 (March 1969), p. 112. For a good, brief statement of the three major ways innovation has been used in previous work see Gerald Zaltman, Robert Duncan, and Jonny Holbek, *Innovations and Organizations* (New York: John Wiley, 1973), pp. 7-16.

[9] For more on this point see Anthony Downs, *Inside Bureaucracy* (Boston: Little Brown, 1967).

[10] Mohr, *op.cit.*, p. 112.

[11] Virginia Gray has recently argued that states vary in their "innovativeness" according to the issue area. Although Nebraska is not usually thought of as an innovative state (and Gray shows that on several measures it is in the bottom one-third of states in innovation), on this issue Nebraska was clearly innovative. See Gray, "Innovation in the States: A Diffusion Study," *American Political Science Review,* 67 (December, 1973), pp. 1174-85.

Notes to Chapter II

[1] For more on Hawaii, see John E. Moore, "The Hawaiian Ombudsman," forthcoming.

[2] Senator Loran Schmit, testimony before Nebraska Legislature, Committee on Judiciary, March 24, 1969.

[3] See Anderson, *Ombudsmen for American Government?*; Walter Gellhorn, *When Americans Complain* (Cambridge: Harvard University Press, 1966); Donald C. Rowat, *The Ombudsman: Citizens' Defender* (Toronto: University of Toronto Press, 1965).

[4] Testimony before Nebraska Legislature, Committee on Judiciary, March 24, 1969.

[5]
> There is hereby created a Legislative Council....which shall consist of all members of the Legislature. It shall be the function of the Legislative Council to consider legislative policies between sessions of the Legislature.... [The Executive Board of the Legislative Council] shall consist of a chairman, vice-chairman, and a member of the Legislature selected at large, the Speaker of the Legislature, and the Chairman of the Committee on Committees of the Legislature.... The Executive Board shall supervise all services and service personnel of the Legislature.

Nebraska, *Revised Statutes*, Secs. 50-401 and 50-401.01.

[6] See Anderson, *Ombudsman Papers*, pp. 28-39, for a discussion of this objection as it was raised in other states.

Notes to Chapter II cont'd.

[7] "The Diffusion of Innovation Among the American States," *American Political Science Review*, 63 (September 1969), p. 897.

[8] Gerald Zaltman, Robert Duncan, and Jonny Holbek, *Innovations and Organizations* (New York: John Wiley, 1973), p. 54.

Notes to Chapter III

[1] Ironically, one of those absent and not voting was Senator Schmit. He was in Honolulu attending the First Annual Ombudsman Workship, sponsored by the Ombudsman Activities Project, University of California, Santa Barbara. For an account of that workshop see Stanley V. Anderson and John E. Moore, eds., *Establishing Ombudsman Offices: Recent Experience in the United States* (Berkeley: Institute of Governmental Studies, University of California, 1972).

[2] During legislative consideration of the Ombudsman bill in Hawaii, it was widely rumored that Herman Doi would receive the first appointment. Because of Doi's fine reputation with legislators, some potential legislative opponents were co-opted by the bill's supporters. See Anderson and Moore, *op. cit.*

[3] OEO's involvement with the Nebraska Ombudsman began as a result of pure happenstance. While then Governor Tiemann was attending a meeting in Washington, D.C., he heard a casual remark to the effect that OEO was interested in funding Ombudsman demonstration projects. Remembering that Nebraska's Ombudsman had not received an appropriation, Tiemann pursued this conversation and before long, OEO was talking to Senator Schmit and others about federal funding.

Notes to Chapter III cont'd

[4] The same editorial took the Executive Board to task for delaying the nomination so long. The newspaper questioned the legislature's sincerity about the Ombudsman office. "The idea of an Ombudsman can work; it can serve a definite public need; and Murrell McNeil can make it so, if he is permitted the opportunity to do so. It will not work if it is to be a plaything of the Legislature or if McNeil is to be regarded as just a handyman for the senators." Lincoln *Star*, May 1971.

[5] McNeil's long tenure in the military bureaucracy and then his service in the public bureaucracy of Nebraska made him sensitive about this issue. To this day, he maintains a determination not to create extra busy-work for bureaucrats and not to impose his own decision rules upon an otherwise reasonable decision.

Notes to Chapter IV

[1] The Nebraska State government telephone book was used as the sampling frame. We assumed--and our assumption was verified by several Nebraska administrators--that the names in the telephone book were middle level and top level management. Every other name was selected, yielding a sample of 218. After one follow-up reminder letter, the response rate was 71 percent (N=156). The respondents appear to be a representative sample by virtue of two features. First, because the telephone book is organized alphabetically by departments, the larger departments were sent more questionnaires than the smaller ones. Second, the response rate indicates that, with the exception of a few small agencies (e.g., Nebraska Arts Council), the proportion of responses from each agency is approximately equal to the total responses. See Appendix II for a copy of the questionnaire.

Notes to Chapter IV cont'd

² When asked what formal procedures their agency has to allow a citizen to lodge a complaint against the agency, almost one-half of the respondents mentioned a procedure that centralized the complaint process. That is, a process was mentioned which directs the aggrieved citizen to a formal hearing board, hearing officer or department head.

³ For more on this subject, see Timothy L. Fitzharris, *The Desirability of a Correctional Ombudsman* (Berkeley: Institute of Governmental Studies, University of California, 1973) and Lance Tibbles, "Ombudsman for American Prisons," *North Dakota Law Review* 48 (Spring 1972), pp. 383-441.

⁴ Almost all the inquiries and complaints received by the governor's office arrive by mail. With certain exceptions, I am confident that the mail I read was a representative sample. It included all of the correspondence for the two weeks prior to my visit. Not included in the mail which was made available was any correspondence of a purely political nature or a complaint or inquiry from a politically prominent individual, correspondence handled personally by the governor.

⁵ The prime reason for lack of follow-up is insufficient staff.

⁶ Not all legislators indicated applicable responses to each question. Therefore, some of the data reported here represent replies from less than 35 Senators (in 1972) or 34 (in 1973). See Appendix III for the text of the questionnaire.

⁷ The number of contacts per week varies enormously. The responses ranged from a low of 2 per week to a high

Notes to Chapter IV cont'd

of 150 per week for in-session contacts, and from a low of 1 to a high of 50 per week for out-of-session contacts.

[8] "Redundancy, Rationality, and the Problem of Duplication and Overlap," *Public Administration Review*, 29 (July-August 1969), pp. 346-358.

[9] *Ibid.*, p. 356.

[10] Landau says, "the probability of failure in a system decreases exponentially as redundancy factors are increased. Increasing reliability in this manner, of course, raises the price to be paid and if fail-safe conditions are to be reached, the cost may be prohibitive. But an immediate corollary of the theorem eases this problem for it requires only arithmetic increases in redundancy to yield geometric increases in reliability. Costs may then be quite manageable." *Ibid.*, p. 350.

Notes to Chapter V

[1] The period covered is slightly longer than two years because McNeil took office on May 1, 1971 and this report evaluates the office to June 30, 1973. The budget figures include an estimate of expenditures for June 1973.

[2] Opening an office in Omaha would have required surmounting some difficult political problems as well. The move could have been interpreted by the 15 Omaha area senators as an "infringement." The monetary side of the issue was more important. The Legislative Council Executive Board recently defeated a proposal to establish offices for Omaha area senators in a newly

Notes to Chapter V cont'd

acquired state office building in downtown Omaha. If the senators were unwilling to open their own offices in Omaha, they might have been suspicious of an attempt by McNeil. As in many other instances, McNeil's political judgment was sound.

[3] McNeil has recently adopted a new form that should give his office more knowledge of agency action on a case. Along with his final letter to a citizen, McNeil includes a self-addressed stamped postcard that asks the citizen to inform him when, if ever, the appropriate agency contacts the citizen. In this way, McNeil can monitor the agencies and their promises.

[4] The Seattle Ombudsman spent three months working on one such investigation. See John E. Moore, "The Seattle Ombudsman," forthcoming.

[5] Lincoln *Star*, January 21, 1972, editorial page.

Notes to Chapter VI

[1] With 70 percent of the combined two-city metropolitan population, Omaha has accounted for 33 percent of the Ombudsman's metropolitan caseload. Lincoln, with 30 percent of the population total, had contributed 67 percent of the metropolitan caseload.

[2] The short turnaround time on cases may mean several other things. For instance, if McNeil is presenting only easily handled requests to the agencies, they can give him quick responses. Short turnaround time may indicate that McNeil does not often disagree with an agency's explanation for its handling of a case; disagreement ususally means further communication with

Notes to Chapter VI cont'd

the agency and, therefore, a loss of time. There is some validity to both of these additional explanations for McNeil's rapid resolution of his cases.

[3] The figures on legislative referrals do not include these kinds of policy research requests from senators.

[4] The number of legislative referrals McNeil received exceeded similar referrals received by the Iowa or Hawaii state Ombudsman.

[5] The British Parliamentary Commissioner for Administration receives complaints only from legislators. See William B. Gwyn, "The British PCA: Ombudsman or Ombudsmouse?" *Journal of Politics,* 35 (1973), pp. 45-69.

[6] Two-hundred-eighty-eight cases required no investigation and were handled in the office, and therefore, no agency was contacted. In 347 cases, the method of investigation was not recorded; it was not possible to ascertain if an investigation was undertaken in 52 cases.

[7] Our examination of the records confirms McNeil's judgment about which cases come from poor individuals.

[8] U.S. Department of Commerce, Bureau of the Census, *General Social and Economic Characteristics: Nebraska,* pp. 29-196.

[9] For a discussion of the Ombudsman's possible relationship to the poor, see John E. Moore, "Ombudsman and the Ghetto" *Connecticut Law Review* 1 (December 1968), pp. 244-262. Moore's footnote references provide a good bibliography on this subject.

Notes to Chapter VI cont'd

[10] *Ibid.*

[11] "Controlling the Bureaucracy of the Antipoverty Program," 31 *Law and Contemporary Problems* (1966), p. 195.

[12] Moore, *op.cit.*

[13] Another alternative would be to give McNeil jurisdiction over local government. This would require the expansion of the Ombudsman's office to handle the additional cases.

Notes to Chapter VIII

[1] Gellhorn, "Annotated Model Ombudsman Statute," in Anderson, *Ombudsmen for American Government?*, pp. 159-173. See Appendix IV for the Nebraska legislation.

[2] Naturally, in the early years of a new institution, its dependence will be greater. Even in seemingly well-established Ombudsman offices, the vicissitudes of politics preclude complete independence of action.

[3] See Chapter IV for a fuller discussion of the survey. Appendix II contains a copy of the questionnaire.

[4] Because few respondents had worked in state government for longer than 20 years, this was chosen as a convenient end point.

Notes to Chapter IX

[1] "The Bureaucracy Problem," *The Public Interest* 6 (Winter 1967), pp. 3-9. The other two problems Wilson identifies are accountability and fiscal integrity.

[2] Wilson, p. 4.

[3] For an article that creates the extreme independence impression, see Donald C. Rowat, "The Spread of the Ombudsman Idea," in Anderson, *Ombudsmen for American Government?* pp. 7-36.

[4] Yet, our evaluation of the Ombudsman's public impact rests on skimpy evidence, and evidence of his impact on agencies comes primarily from the perceptions of legislators and administrators. More research is clearly in order.

APPENDIX I

Figures and Tables

Figures
1. Nebraska Ombudsman's Total Caseload,
   May 1971-June 1973.......................... 121
2. Complaints and Inquiries Received,
   May 1971-June 1973.......................... 122
3. Geographic Origin of Caseload,
   May 1971-June 1973.......................... 123

Tables
2. Categories of Cases, May 1971-June 1973....... 124
3. Complaint Type: Jurisdiction and No-
   Jurisdiction, May 1971-June 1973............ 125
4. Complaint Type and Level of Justification,
   May 1971-June 1973.......................... 126
5. No-Jurisdiction Cases Related to Governmental Unit 127
6. Geographic Origin of Ombudsman's Caseload,
   May 1971-June 1973, Compared with
   Nebraska Population......................... 128
7. Elapsed Time: Receipt to Case Close,
   May 1971-June 1973.......................... 129
8. Categories of Cases, Poor and Not-Poor
   Citizens, May 1971-June 1973................ 130
9. Complaint Type: Jurisdiction and No-
   Jurisdiction, for Poor and Not-Poor,
   May 1971-June 1973.......................... 131
10. Elapsed Time: Receipt to Case Close, for
    Poor and Not-Poor, May 1971-June 1973 132

11. Nebraska Legislators' Responses Concerning
    the Ombudsman, July 1972 and July 1973...... 133
12. Nebraska State Administrators' Responses
    Concerning the Ombudsman, July 1973......... 135

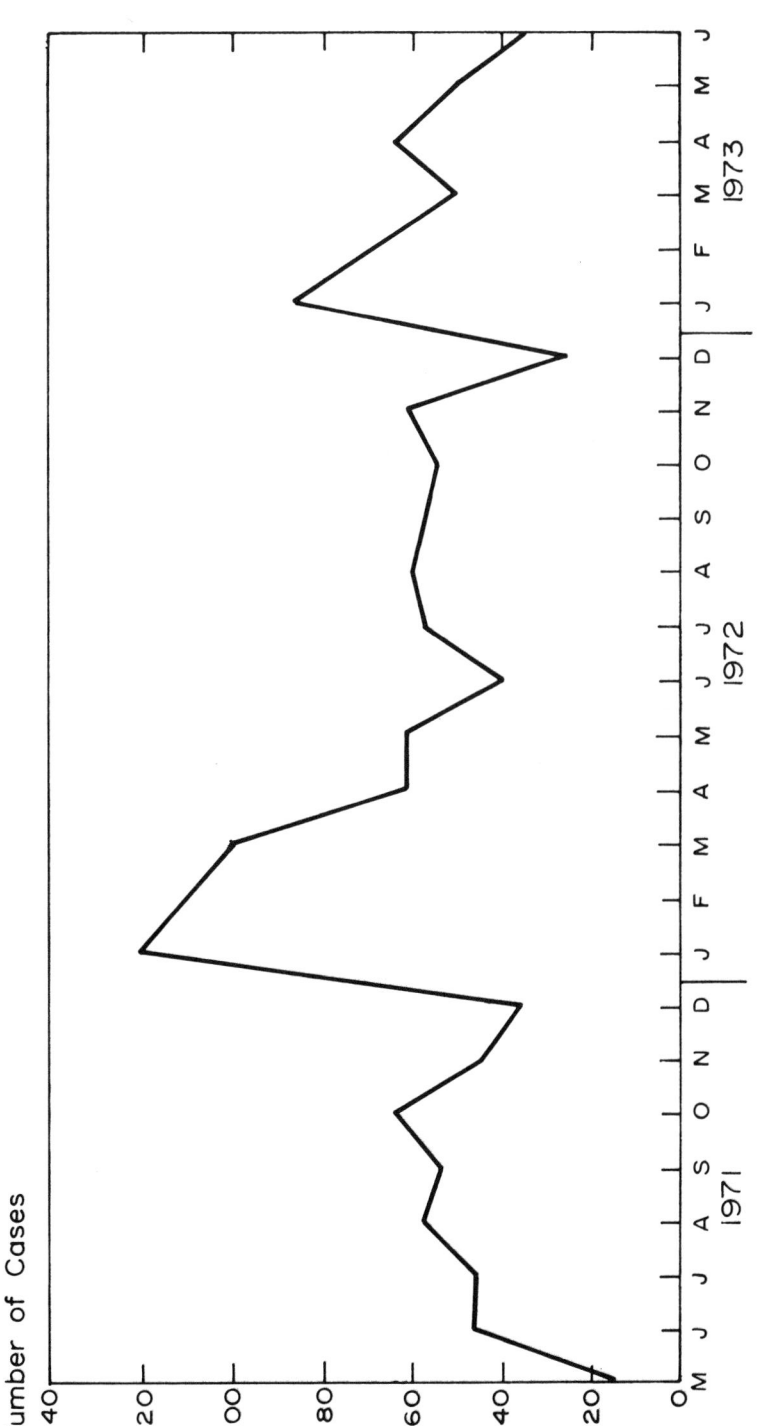

Figure 1

Nebraska Ombudsman's Total Caseload, May 1971-June 1973

Figure 2

Complaints and Inquiries Received, May 1971-June 1973

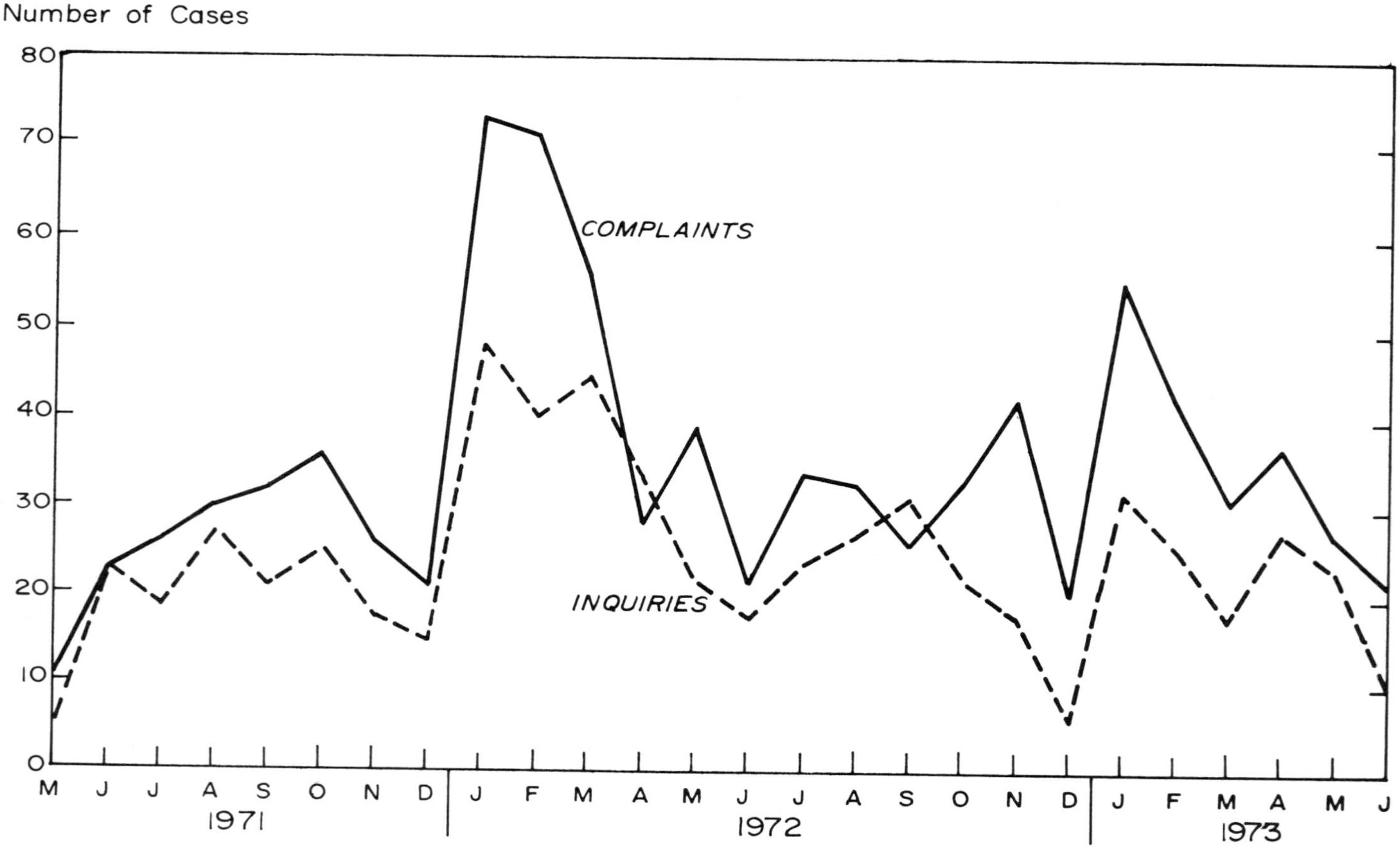

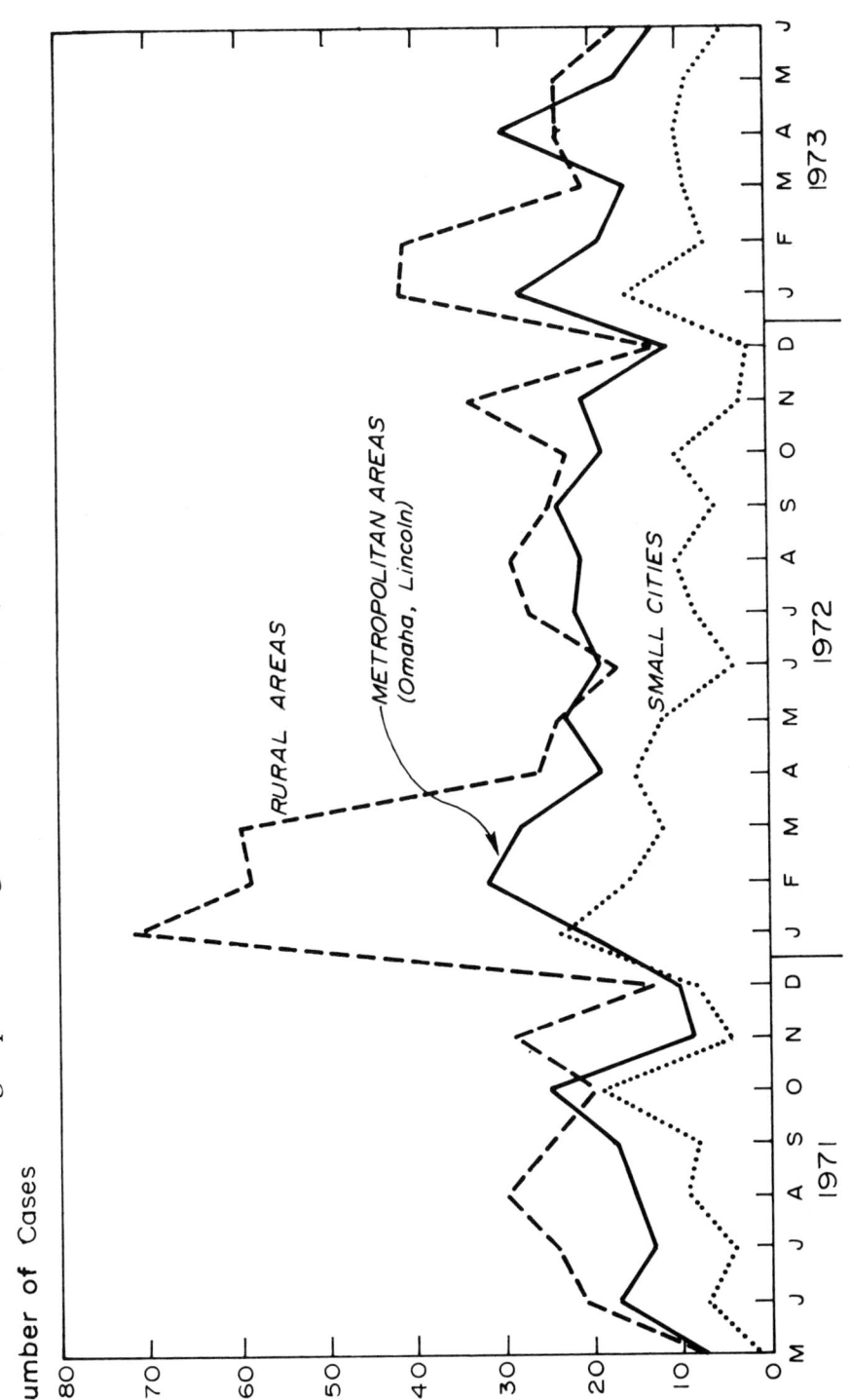

Figure 3

Geographic Origin of Caseload, May 1971-June 1973

Table 2

Categories of Cases,
May 1971 through June 1973

Complaint				
Jurisdiction				
Justified	13.1			
Partially justified	4.9	33.3%	(N=	509)
Unjustified	15.3			
No-jurisdiction				
Assistance	20.9			
No assistance	4.4	25.3	(N=	386)
Inquiry				
Jurisdiction	29.0	29.0	(N=	443)
No-jurisdiction				
Assistance	10.3			
No assistance	1.4	11.7	(N=	179)
Not recorded	0.6	0.6	(N=	9)
TOTALS		99.9%[a]	(N=1,526)	

[a] On this and subsequent tables, percentages may not total 100, because of rounding.

Table 3

Complaint Type:
Jurisdiction and No-Jurisdiction,
May 1971 through June 1973[a]

Complaint type	Jurisdiction	No-jurisdiction	Total
Adequacy of administrative procedure	36.9%	17.4%	28.5%
Appropriateness of administrative opinion	24.8	22.3	23.8
Dispute about the facts of a case	1.7	0.0	1.0
Inadequate or unfair law	9.5	17.1	12.8
Misconduct of officials	7.4	10.9	8.9
Inadequate administrative communication	14.0	2.3	9.0
Consumer	2.1	8.3	4.8
Private dispute or legal matter	1.2	17.1	8.0
Other	2.3	4.7	3.3
	99.9% (N=515)	100.1% (N=386)	100.1% (N=901)

[a] The classification scheme for type of complaints is adapted from Loren L. Mall, "Colorado's Ombudsman Office," 45 *Denver Law Journal* (Winter 1968), p. 132.

Table 4

Complaint Type and Level of Justification,
May 1971 through June 1973

Complaint type	Justified	Partially justified	Un-justified	No-jurisdiction, No-assistance	No-jurisdiction, assistance	Total recorded cases	Not recorded
Adequacy of administrative procedure	43.5%	30.7%	33.8%	9.0%	19.1%	28.5%	22.2%
Appropriateness of administrative opinion	15.0	18.7	35.5	25.4	21.6	23.8	22.2
Dispute about the facts	1.5	0.0	2.6	0.0	0.0	1.0	0.0
Inadequate or unfair law	6.5	10.7	12.0	13.4	17.9	12.8	11.1
Misconduct of officials	7.0	8.0	7.7	10.4	11.0	8.9	0.0
Inadequate administrative communication	20.5	29.3	3.8	0.0	2.8	9.0	0.0
Consumer complaint	1.0	2.7	1.7	10.4	7.8	4.8	33.3
Private legal matter	2.5	0.0	0.0	25.4	15.4	8.0	11.1
Other	2.5	0.0	3.0	6.0	4.4	3.3	0.0
TOTAL	100 % (N=200)	100.1% (N= 75)	100.1% (N=234)	100 % (N= 67)	100 % (N=319)	100.1% (N=892)	99.9% (N= 9)

Table 5

No-Jurisdiction Cases
Related to Governmental Unit

Governmental unit	Percentage
Federal government	17.8%
Nebraska local government	37.8
Governor	0.2
Legislature	10.6
Courts	9.0
Private matters and others	24.6
TOTAL	100 % (N=566)

Table 6

Geographic Origin of
Ombudsman's Caseload
May 1971 through June 1973,
Compared with Nebraska Population

Origin of cases	Percentage of cases[a]	Percentage of population
Metropolitan area: Lincoln and Omaha	33.5%	33.5%
Small cities:[b] Grand Island, Hastings, North Platte, Kearney, Norfolk, Columbus, Scottsbluff, and Beatrice	16.1	11.8
Rural areas	50.4	54.7
TOTAL	100 % (N=1,480)	100 % (N=1,483,493)

[a] Excluding 46 "Not recorded" or "Out of state" cases.

[b] All cities above 10,000 people were included, except Lincoln and Omaha.

Table 7

Elapsed Time: Receipt to Case CLose,
May 1971 through June 1973

	Complaints		Inquiries		
Number of days from receipt to close	Jurisdiction	No-jurisdiction	Jurisdiction	No-jurisdiction	Total
1-3	39.7%	59.1%	67.0%	73.7%	56.6%
4-7	20.6	19.7	19.2	11.7	18.9
8-14	15.9	10.9	9.5	8.4	11.9
15-21	6.3	4.1	1.4	1.7	3.8
22-30	6.1	2.1	1.1	1.1	3.0
31-90	8.6	2.3	1.4	1.7	4.4
Over 90	1.6	0.8	0.2	0.6	0.6
Open or discontinued	1.2	1.0	0.2	1.1	0.8
TOTAL	100 % (N=509)	100 % (N=386)	100 % (N=443)	100 % (N=179)	100 % (N=1,517)[a]

[a] Excluding 9 "Not recorded" cases.

Table 8

Categories of Cases,
Poor and Not-Poor Citizens,
May 1971 through June 1973

	Economic class		
Type of case	Poor	Not-poor	Total
Complaint			
Jurisdiction			
Justified	12.4%	13.2%	13.1%
Partially justified	4.5	5.0	4.9
Unjustified	26.1	14.1	15.3
No-jurisdiction			
Assistance	22.2	20.8	20.9
No assistance	3.3	4.5	4.4
Inquiry			
Jurisdiction	20.3	30.0	29.0
No-jurisdiction			
Assistance	9.2	10.4	10.3
No assistance	1.3	1.4	1.4
Not recorded	0.6	0.6	0.6
TOTAL	99.9%	100 %	99.9%
	(N=153)	(N=1,373)	(N=1,526)

Table 9

Complaint Type:
Jurisdiction and No-Jurisdiction,
for Poor and Not-Poor,
May 1971 through June 1973

Complaint type	Economic class		Total
	Poor	Not-poor	
Adequacy of administrative procedure	29.2%	28.4%	28.5%
Appropriateness of administrative opinion	32.1	22.6	23.8
Dispute about the facts	1.9	0.9	1.0
Inadequate or unfair law	9.4	13.2	12.8
Misconduct of officials	9.4	8.8	8.9
Inadequate administrative communication	6.6	9.3	9.0
Consumer complaint	0.0	5.5	4.9
Private legal matter	7.5	8.1	8.0
Other	3.8	3.1	3.2
TOTAL	99.9% (N=106)	99.9% (N=795)	100.1% (N=901)

Table 10

Elapsed Time:
Receipt to Case Close,
for Poor and Not-Poor,
May 1971 through June 1973

Number of days to close case	Economic class		Total
	Poor	Not-poor	
1-3	51.0%	57.0%	56.4%
4-7	17.0	19.1	18.9
8-14	11.1	11.9	11.8
15-21	3.9	3.7	3.7
22-30	7.8	2.5	3.1
31-90	5.2	4.2	4.3
Over 90	2.6	0.6	0.8
Open or discontinued cases	1.3	1.0	1.0
TOTAL	99.9% (N=153)	100 % (N=1,373)	100 % (N=1,526)

Table 11

Nebraska Legislators' Responses
Concerning the Ombudsman,
July 1972 and July 1973

What is your impression of the quality of service which the Ombudsman's office provided on those cases which you referred to the office?

	1972	1973
Very good	30	32
Good	2	-
Adequate	1	1
Poor	-	-
Very poor	-	-
No basis to judge	2	-
	(35)	(33)

What is your general impression of the Ombudsman's office?

	1972	1973
Very favorable	26	30
Favorable	7	2
Unfavorable	-	1
Very unfavorable	-	1
No basis to judge	2	-
	(35)	(34)

Generally speaking, one important goal of the Ombudsman institution is improving the administration and implemention of state laws. In your opinion, has the Nebraska Ombudsman:

	1973
Encouraged significant improvement in state government administrative agencies	17

Encouraged some improvement
in state government administrative
agencies 14

Had little or no impact
on state government administrative
agencies 3

In some way, hindered
state government administrative
agencies -

Seriously hindered
state government administrative
agencies -

(34)

(This question was not asked in 1972)

Table 12

Nebraska
State Administrators' Responses
Concerning the Ombudsman
July 1973

1. Do you approve of the Ombudsman idea in general; do you think it is a good idea or not?

Approve strongly	59.6%
Approve	34.6
Disapprove	0.6
Disapprove strongly	0.0
Undecided	5.2
	100 % (N=156)

2. Do you feel that there is a need for an Ombudsman in Nebraska?

Definitely yes	53.2%
Yes	37.2
No	0.6
Definitely no	0.0
Uncertain	8.3
No response	0.7
	100 % (N=156)

3. Should the Nebraska Ombudsman's office become a permanent part of state government?

Yes	84.6%
No	0.0
Uncertain	14.7
No response	0.7
	100 % (N=156)

4. Has the Ombudsman had any effect on policy in your department?

Yes	5.8%
No	89.7
Don't know	2.6
No response	1.9
	100 % (N=156)

5. Generally speaking, one important goal of the Ombudsman institution is improving the administration and implementation of state laws. In your opinion, has the Nebraska Ombudsman:

Encouraged significant improvements in state government administrative agencies	10.9%
Encouraged some improvements in state government administrative agencies	55.8
Had little or no impact on state government administrative agencies	17.3
In some way hindered state government administrative agencies	0.0
Seriously hindered state government administrative agencies	0.0
Don't know	10.3
No response	5.8
	100.1% (N=156)

APPENDIX II
Administrative Personnel Questionnaire

Ombudsman Activities Project
Administrative Personnel Questionnaire

1. First of all, how many years have you worked for the state government?
   _____ years

2. How many years have you been in your present position?
   _____ years

3. In your view, which one of the following statements most accurately describes the opinions of Nebraskans *toward your agency*?

   (1) Citizens feel we are doing a *very good* job of administering state laws _____

   (2) Citizens feel we are doing an *adequate* job of administering state laws _____

   (3) Citizens *have no opinions* about the quality of our job performance _____

   (4) Citizens feel we are doing a *poor* job of administering state laws _____

   (5) Citizens feel we are doing a *very poor* job of administering state laws _____

4. In your view, which one of the following statements most accurately describes the opinions of Nebraskans *toward all administrative agencies* in general?

   (1) Citizens feel they are doing a *very good* job of administering state laws _____

   (2) Citizens feel they are doing an *adequate* job of administering state laws _____

   (3) Citizens *have no opinions* about the quality of their job performance _____

(4) Citizens feel they are doing a *poor* job of administering state laws _____

(5) Citizens feel they are doing a *very poor* job of administering state laws _____

5. In your job, approximately how much contact do you have with the public? ("Contact" includes anything from meeting personally with a citizen to writing a letter to a citizen.) Please circle the approximate percentage of "contact" out of your total working time, taking an average of the last year.

   0% 10 20 30 40 50 60 70 80 90 100%

6. Thinking of all your contacts with the public, please check which method of contact in which you engage most frequently.

   (1) Face to face, personal contact _____
   (2) Telephone contact _____
   (3) Letters _____
   (4) Other _____

7. Approximately what percentage of your contacts with the public involve complaints from citizens?

   0% 10 20 30 40 50 60 70 80 90 100%

8. Of the complaints you receive from the public, approximately what percentage are valid and justified in the sense that an error has been made or an individual has been treated improperly?

   0% 10 20 30 40 50 60 70 80 90 100%

9. What formal procedures, if any, does your agency have to allow a citizen to lodge a complaint against a decision made by the agency?
   _____

9a. In your opinion, are these procedures adequate?

Yes, because _____

No, because _____

10. In your opinion, what do the citizens who register complaints with your agency feel about the agency's complaint handling procedures?

    (1) Complaint handling procedures are *very good* _____

    (2) Complaint handling procedures are *adequate* _____

    (3) Complaint handling procedures are *poor* _____

    (4) Complaint handling procedures are *very poor* _____

    (5) No basis to judge citizens' reactions _____

IN THIS SECTION, WE ARE INTERESTED IN YOUR REACTIONS TO THE OPERATIONS OF THE NEBRASKA OMBUDSMAN.

11. Prior to receiving this questionnaire, were you aware that Nebraska has a state Ombudsman?

    (1) Yes _____

    (2) No _____

12. In your view, what are the Ombudsman's basic functions?

_____

_____

13. Do you approve of the Ombudsman idea in general; do you think it is a good idea or not?

    (1) Approve strongly _____

(2) Approve
(3) Disapprove
(4) Disapprove strongly
(5) Undecided

14. Do you feel that there is a need for an Ombudsman in Nebraska?

    (1) Definitely yes
    (2) Yes
    (3) No
    (4) Definitely no
    (5) Uncertain

15. What general impression have you gained of the Ombudsman (his work, the way he performs his functions, etc.)?

    (1) Very positive
    (2) Somewhat positive
    (3) Somewhat negative
    (4) Very negative
    (5) Uncertain

16. Do you know the Ombudsman personally?

    (1) Yes
    (2) No

17. How many times, if any, has the Ombudsman's office contacted you about a complaint or question brought to the Ombudsman?

    (1) Not at all
    (2) 1-3 times

(3) 4-6 times _____
(4) 7-10 times _____
(5) 11-12 times _____
(6) More than 12 times _____

18. Have you ever been in a situation where you were dealing with a citizen and you thought he might send a complaint to the Ombudsman?

    (1) Yes _____
    (2) No _____
    (3) Uncertain _____

    18a. If yes to Question 18: In what way, if any, did the possibility of the citizen contacting the Ombudsman affect your handling of the case?

    _____

    _____

19. In your opinion, has the Ombudsman had any effect on *policy* in your department, i.e., have policies been reconsidered or changed in the light of the Ombudsman's activities?

    _____

    _____

20. Have any special directives (written or verbal) about the Ombudsman been circulated in your department?

    (1) Yes _____
    (2) No _____
    (3) Don't know _____

20a. If yes to Question 20: Would you please specify your interpretation of these directives (formal or informal), i.e., what the directives expect you to do.

_____

_____

21. Do you think that changes should be made in the jurisdiction or operation of the Ombudsman?

    (1) Yes   _____
    (2) No   _____
    (3) Uncertain _____

    21a. If yes to Question 21: Would you please specify which changes you personally think are desirable.

    _____

    _____

22. All things considered, should the Nebraska Ombudsman's office become a permanent part of state government?

    (1) Yes   _____
    (2) No   _____
    (3) Uncertain _____

23. Generally speaking, one important goal of the Ombudsman institution is improving the administration and implementation of state laws. In your opinion, has the Nebraska Ombudsman:

    (1) Encouraged significant improvements in state government administrative agencies? _____

(2) Encouraged some improvements in state government administrative agencies? _____

(3) Had little or no impact on state government administrative agencies? _____

(4) In some way, hindered state government administrative agencies? _____

(5) Seriously hindered state government administrative agencies? _____

APPENDIX III
Nebraska Legislature Questionnaire

Ombudsman Activities Project
Nebraska Legislature Questionnaire

1. How many contacts would you estimate that you receive from your constituents?

    Number per week: When legislature is in
    session   _____
    When legislature is not
    in session   _____

2. What is the nature of the contacts you receive from your constituents?

    Approximate percent that are:
    Opinions on issues or suggestions for
      legislation   ____%
    Requests for information   ____%
    Complaints about state government   ____%
    Other (please specify) _____   ____%

3. What are the most common types of complaints that you receive?

    a. _____
    b. _____
    c. _____

4. Considering your experience in investigating constituents' complaints about state government, approximately what percent of such complaints do you feel have been valid and justified in the sense that an error has been made or an individual has been treated improperly?

    Percent of complaints that are valid: ____%

5. Since July 1, 1972, have you personally referred any of your constituents' complaints or questions to the Nebraska Ombudsman?

   Yes _____   No _____

   If 'yes' on (5):

   a. About how many cases have you referred? _____

   b. What is your impression of the quality of service which the Ombudsman's office provided on those cases?

      Very good   _____
      Good   _____
      Adequate   _____
      Poor   _____
      Very poor   _____
      No basis to judge _____

6. What is your impression of the Ombudsman's office?

      Very favorable   _____
      Favorable   _____
      Unfavorable   _____
      Very unfavorable _____
      No basis to judge _____

7. In your opinion, what (if anything) should the Ombudsman's office do to further improve the quality of its service?

   _____
   _____
   _____

8. Generally speaking, one important goal of the Ombudsman institution is improving the administration and implementation of state laws. In your opinion, has the Nebraska Ombudsman:

   Encouraged significant improvement in state government administrative agencies? _____

   Encouraged some improvement in state government administrative agencies? _____

   Had little or no impact on state government administrative agencies? _____

   In some way, hindered state government administrative agencies? _____

   Seriously hindered state government administrative agencies? _____

9. Do you have any general comments on these questions which might more fully explain your answers?

APPENDIX IV

Legislative Bill 521: Public Counsel

Legislative Bill 521

(Final form sent to printer July 17, 1969)

A BILL

FOR AN ACT relating to state government; to create the office of Public Counsel; to provide powers, duties, and qualifications; to make certain acts unlawful; and to provide a penalty.

Be it enacted by the people of the State of Nebraska,

Sec. 1. As used in this act, unless the context otherwise requires:

(1) Administrative agency shall mean any department, board, commission, or other governmental unit, any official, or any employee of the State of Nebraska acting or purporting to act by reason of connection with the State of Nebraska; but shall not include (a) any court, (b) any member or employee of the Legislature or the Legislative Council, (c) the Governor or his personal staff, (d) any political subdivision or entity thereof, (e) any instrumentality formed pursuant to an interstate compact and answerable to more than one state, or (f) any entity of the federal government; and

(2) Administrative act shall include every action, rule, regulation, order, omission, decision, recommendation, practice, or procedure of an administrative agency.

Sec. 2. The office of Public Counsel is hereby established to exercise the authority and perform the duties provided by this act. The Public Counsel shall be appointed by the Legislature, with the vote of two-thirds of the members required for approval of such appointment from nominations submitted by the Executive Board of the Legislative Council.

Sec. 3. The Public Counsel shall be a person well equipped to analyze problems of law, administration, and public policy, and during his term of office shall not be actively involved in partisan affairs. No person may serve as Public Counsel within two years of the last day on which he served as a member of the Legislature, or while he is a candidate for or holds any other state office, or while he is engaged in any other occupation for reward or profit.

Sec. 4. The Public Counsel shall serve for a term of six years, unless removed by vote of two-thirds of the members of the Legislature upon their determining that he has become incapacitated or has been guilty of neglect of duty or misconduct. If the office of Public Counsel becomes vacant for any cause, the deputy public counsel shall serve as acting public counsel until a Public Counsel has been appointed for a full term. The Public Counsel shall receive such salary as is set by the Executive Board of the Legislative Council.

Sec. 5. The Public Counsel may select, appoint, and compensate as he may see fit, within the amount available by appropriation, such assistants and employees as he may deem necessary to discharge his responsibilities under this act, and shall designate one of his assistants to be the deputy public counsel. The Public Counsel may delegate to members of his staff any of his authority or duty under this act except the power of delegation and the duty of formally making recommendations to administrative agencies or reports to the Governor or the Legislature.

Sec. 6. The Public Counsel shall have the following powers:

(1) He may investigate, on complaint or on his own motion, any administrative act of any administrative agency;

(2) He may prescribe the methods by which complaints are to be made, received, and acted upon; he

may determine the scope and manner of investigations to be made; and, subject to the requirements of this act, he may determine the form, frequency, and distribution of his conclusions, recommendations, and proposals;

(3) He may request and shall be given by each administrative agency the assistance and information he deems necessary for the discharge of his responsibilities; he may inspect and examine the records and documents of all administrative agencies; and he may enter and inspect premises within any administrative agency's control;

(4) He may issue a subpoena, enforceable by action in an appropriate court, to compel any person to appear, give sworn testimony, or produce documentary or other evidence he deems relevant to a matter under his inquiry. A person thus required to provide information shall be paid the same fees and travel allowances and shall be accorded the same privileges and immunities as are extended to witnesses in the district courts of this state, and shall also be entitled to have counsel present while being questioned; and

(5) He may undertake, participate in, or cooperate with general studies or inquiries, whether or not related to any particular administrative agency or any particular administrative act, if he believes that they may enhance knowledge about or lead to improvements in the functioning of administrative agencies.

Sec. 7. In selecting matters for his attention, the Public Counsel shall address himself particularly to an administrative act that might be:

(1) Contrary to law or regulation;

(2) Unreasonable, unfair, oppressive, or inconsistent with the general course of an administrative agency's judgments;

(3) Mistaken in law or arbitrary in ascertainments of fact;

     (4) Improper in motivation or based on irrelevant considerations;

     (5) Unclear or inadequately explained when reasons should have been revealed; or

     (6) Inefficiently performed.

The Public Counsel may concern himself also with strengthening procedures and practices which lessen the risk that objectionable administrative acts will occur.

     Sec. 8. The Public Counsel may receive a complaint from any person concerning an administrative act. He shall conduct a suitable investigation into the things complained of unless he believes that:

     (1) The complainant has available to him another remedy which he could reasonably be expected to use;

     (2) The grievance pertains to a matter outside his power;

     (3) The complainant's interest is insufficiently related to the subject matter;

     (4) The complaint is trivial, frivolous, vexatious, or not made in good faith;

     (5) Other complaints are more worthy of attention;

     (6) His resources are insufficient for adequate investigation; or

     (7) The complaint has been too long delayed to justify present examination of its merit.

The Public Counsel's declining to investigate a complaint shall not bar him from proceeding on his own motion to inquire into related problems. After completing his consideration of a complaint, whether or not it has been investigated, the Public Counsel shall suitably inform the complainant and the administrative agency involved.

Sec. 9. Before announcing a conclusion or recommendation that expressly or impliedly criticizes an administrative agency or any person, the Public Counsel shall consult with that agency or person.

Sec. 10. (1) If, having considered a complaint and whatever material he deems pertinent, the Public Counsel is of the opinion that an administrative agency should (a) consider the matter further, (b) modify or cancel an administrative act, (c) alter a regulation or ruling, (d) explain more fully the administrative act in question, or (e) take any other step, he shall state his recommendations to the administrative agency. If the Public Counsel so requests, the agency shall, within the time he has specified, inform him about the action taken on his recommendations or the reasons for not complying with them.

(2) If the Public Counsel believes that an administrative action has been dictated by a statute whose results are unfair or otherwise objectionable, he shall bring to the Legislature's notice his views concerning desirable statutory change.

Sec. 11. The Public Counsel may publish his conclusions and suggestions by transmitting them to the Governor, the Legislature or any of its committees, the press, and others who may be concerned. When publishing an opinion adverse to an administrative agency he shall include any statement the administrative agency may have made to him by way of explaining its past difficulties or its present rejection of the Public Counsel's proposals.

Sec. 12. In addition to whatever reports he may make from time to time, the Public Counsel shall on or about February 15 of each year report to the Legislature and to the Governor concerning the exercise of his functions during the preceding calendar year. In discussing matters with which he has dealt, the Public Counsel need not identify those immediately concerned if to do so would cause needless hardship. So far as the annual report may criticize named agencies or officials, it must include also their replies to the criticism.

Sec. 13. If the Public Counsel has reason to believe that any public officer or employee has acted in a manner warranting criminal or disciplinary proceedings, he shall refer the matter to the appropriate authorities.

Sec. 14. No proceeding, opinion, or expression of the Public Counsel shall be reviewable in any court. Neither the Public Counsel nor any member of his staff shall be required to testify or produce evidence in any judicial or administrative proceeding concerning matters within his official cognizance, except in a proceeding brought to enforce this act.

Sec. 15. A person who willfully obstructs or hinders the proper exercise of the Public Counsel's functions, or who willfully misleads or attempts to mislead the Public Counsel in his inquiries, shall be guilty of a misdemeanor and, upon conviction thereof, shall be fined not more than one thousand dollars. No employee of the State of Nebraska, who files a complaint pursuant to this act, shall be subject to any penalties, sanctions, or restrictions in connection with his employment because of such complaint.

INSTITUTE OF GOVERNMENTAL STUDIES
109 Moses Hall, University of California
Berkeley, California 94720

OMBUDSMAN RESEARCH

Monographs

Mikael Hidén
The Ombudsman in Finland: The First Fifty Years. 198pp 1973 $8.00

Kent M. Weeks
Ombudsmen Around the World: A Comparative Chart. 101pp 1973 $3.00

Alan J. Wyner, ed.
Executive Ombudsmen in the United States. 315pp 1973 $5.50

Timothy L. Fitzharris
The Desirability of a Correctional Ombudsman. 114pp 1973 $3.00

Stanley V. Anderson and John E. Moore, eds.
Establishing Ombudsman Offices: Recent Experience in the United States. 293pp 1972 $3.00

Lance Tibbles and John H. Hollands
Buffalo Citizens Administrative Service: An Ombudsman Demonstration Project. 90pp 1970 $2.75

Stanley V. Anderson
Ombudsman Papers: American Experience and Proposals. 407pp 1969 $3.75

Stanley Scott, ed.
Western American Assembly on the Ombudsman: Report. 36pp 1968 $1.00

Dean Mann
The Citizen and the Bureaucracy: Complaint-Handling Procedures of Three California Legislators. 52pp 1968 $1.25

Stanley V. Anderson
Canadian Ombudsman Proposals. 168pp 1966 $2.50

California residents add 6 percent sales tax; residents of Alameda, Contra Costa and San Francisco counties add 6½ percent sales tax. Prepay orders under $10.00.

Public Affairs Reports

Alan J. Wyner
"Lieutenant Governors as Political Ombudsmen." v. 12, no. 6, 1971

Carl E. Schwarz
"The Mexican Writ of Amparo: An Extraordinary Remedy Against Official Abuse of Individual Rights: Part I." v. 10, no. 6, 1969; and Part II, v. 11, no. 1, 1970.

Stanley V. Anderson
"Ombudsman Proposals: Stimulus to Inquiry." v. 7, no. 6, 1966   4pp
"The Ombudsman: Public Defender Against Maladministration." v. 6, no. 2, 1965   4pp

Public Affairs Reports are now available in collected volumes; *Emerging Issues in Public Policy: Research Reports and Essays.* The 1960–1965 volume and the 1966–1972 volume are $11.00 each.

Reprints

John E. Moore
"Ombudsman and the Ghetto," 1 *Connecticut Law Review* (2)   December 1968   (IGS Reprint #39)

Lance Tibbles
"Ombudsmen for American Prisons," 48 *North Dakota Law Review* (3)   Spring 1972   (IGS Reprint #44)